One-on-One Training

One-on-One Training

How to Effectively Train One Person at a Time

Bob Pike, CSP, CPAE
Lynn Solem
Dave Arch

Jossey-Bass
Pfeiffer
San Francisco

Creative Training Techniques
International, Inc.

Copyright © 2000 by Jossey-Bass/Pfeiffer and Creative Training Techniques Press

ISBN: 0-7879-5143-9

Library of Congress Cataloging-in-Publication Data
Arch, Dave.
  One-on-one training : how to effectively train one person at
a time / Dave Arch, Bob Pike, Lynn Solem.
    p. cm.
  Includes bibliographical references.
  ISBN 0-7879-5143-9
  1. Employees—Training of. I. Pike, Bob, 1947-
II. Solem, Lynn, 1934- III. Title.
HF5549.5.T7 A716 2000
658.3'124—dc   99-6639

Printed in the United States of America

Published by

 350 Sansome Street, 5th Floor
San Francisco, California 94104-1342
(415) 433-1740; Fax (415) 433-0499
(800) 274-4434; Fax (800) 569-0443

7620 West 78th Street
Minneapolis, MN 55439
(800) 383-9210
(612) 829-1954; Fax (612) 829-0260

Visit our website at: http://www.pfeiffer.com

Visit our website at:
http://www.creativetrainingtech.com

Acquiring Editor: Matthew Holt
Director of Development: Kathleen Dolan-Davies
Developmental Editor: Rebecca Taff
Senior Production Editor: Dawn Kilgore
Manufacturing Supervisor: Becky Carreño

Printing 10 9 8 7 6 5 4 3 2 1

This book is printed on acid-free, recycled stock that meets or exceeds the minimum GPO and EPA requirements for recycled paper.

Contents

Introduction

Two kinds of trainers are looking for new one-on-one techniques: those who currently train one-on-one and are looking for new approaches and those who previously have trained only in classroom settings and are now switching to one-on-one training.

The use of one-on-one training is increasing in many organizations for three primary reasons: (1) Classroom training is expensive, and on many occasions the number of people needed to make up a class in order to maximize the value of the expenditure is not available; (2) New hires often come on board one at a time and cannot wait to be trained; and (3) Often the most appropriate way for the learner to be taught is on the job itself.

Three Forms of Training

One-on-one training usually takes one of three forms: (1) A company trainer or manager sits down with a new hire and explains policies and/or procedures or delivers some kind of information; (2) A trainer or supervisor works with a learner to teach that learner a skill, such as how to operate a piece of equipment or use a certain software program; or (3) A non-trainer, often a peer or colleague, works at his or her job while training someone else to do that job. This book is designed to be used in any of these situations, although to be less cumbersome, we have addressed it simply to "you," the trainer—whatever your function.

Training a group in a classroom and training one person in a non-classroom setting call for different types of skills. Trainers who rely on group involvement and interaction to create a "learning moment" can be at a loss when it comes to training one person. If you are such a trainer, you may want information on involvement techniques for one-on-one training; on gauging retention; measuring comprehension; creating a safe environment; and so forth. This book is for you.

Changes Driving Training Industry

Let's look at some of the changes that are driving today's training industry. In the February 10, 1997, issue of *USA Today*, on the front page of the Money section, was an article announcing that the Federal government was going to pilot a pay-for-performance system with certain segments of its workforce. "Pay-for-performance" is a system whereby jobs are broken down into component parts and criteria are set for employees' performance of each of those parts. Promotions and professional growth are based on how well individuals perform the job. If you are the one responsible for training someone to meet measurable standards under these circumstances, you naturally want to make sure that the individual is thoroughly trained.

According to *USA Today*, no public corporations were utilizing pay-for-performance strategies as recently as 1990, but 33⅓ percent were as of the date of the article. It's not difficult to spot a trend here. Trainers who specialize in performance troubleshooting are going to be in great demand.

You may find that you are more valuable to your organization doing one-on-one training than you are in the classroom—and even more valuable when you are training line managers, supervisors, and subject-matter experts on how to do one-on-one training. This book includes techniques that apply to both of these situations. We suggest that you give copies to those you are training so that they can apply the techniques themselves.

A traditional trainer's job description might look like this:

✓ Assess training needs;

✓ Design training;

✓ Deliver training; and

✓ Measure impact of training.

A new job description might include:

✓ Stay in touch with workers and work process to be aware of skill needs;

✓ Teach line managers how to train others; and

✓ Facilitate process improvement and/or teach line managers how to do it.

Prophets of doom are saying the training field is going to disappear, but whether we agree with that or not, we do know that—just as those in the classroom must be lifetime learners—so must we as trainers accept our changing organizational roles. It could be that trainers for the year 2000 and beyond will have to serve more organizational business needs than they have in the past. In fact, we are surely in for a re-engineering of what training is all about. As we teach line managers and others to do on-the-job training, we will be expected to help them to be successful. Knowing as much as we can about one-on-one techniques can help ensure our success.

This book was written for anyone undertaking to train someone else in a one-on-one setting, whether experienced classroom trainer or manager teaching skills to employees, whether peer or colleague or company trainer with a large repertoire of methods. The material in Section 1 on adult learning (Chapter 1) and on designing training (Chapter 2), along with the techniques in Section 2 should allow you to be the best you can be.

Section 1

SPECIAL ASPECTS OF ONE-ON-ONE TRAINING

Because you are training adults, you must consider their needs. To help you with this, we have provided a chapter on the Principles of Adult Learning, laid out in four easy-to-remember segments with some hints for incorporating them into your design.

We've also provided a chapter on An Eight-Step Process for Designing Training that is also applicable for one-on-one situations.

CHAPTER 1

Principles of Adult Learning

No matter what the setting, your training endeavors will be more successful if you build in the four Principles of Adult Learning (Kodak Institute, 1989). You have undoubtedly built the principles into your classroom settings if you have experience with classroom training, and now you need techniques to ensure that they are incorporated into your one-on-one training also. Briefly, the four are: (1) Adults must be viewed as individuals for learning to be effective; (2) Adults want to be involved actively in their own learning; (3) What adults are taught must be perceived as useful; and (4) Adult learning must be reinforced immediately. Let's look at each principle individually.

Principle 1: Adults Must Be Viewed As Individuals

For learning to be effective, adults must be seen as individuals. Individuality includes three subcategories:

✓ *Self-Concept:* The acknowledgment of the trainee's feelings, values, attitudes, and expectations;

✓ *Comfort Level:* Both physical and psychological levels of comfort with the training situation; and

✓ *Past Experience:* An acknowledgment of the trainee's past experiences.

These components of the first principle can be easily incorporated into the learning experience. The rewards are increased buy-in, higher motivation, feelings of self-esteem, and enhanced retention. If you are training line managers to do on-the-job training, you will want to make sure that they have the information they need to treat their learners as individuals.

Bonus Technique

Here's a way to help reduce tension and build rapport at the beginning of a training program. Start a flip-chart sheet to collect personal data. Draw a line vertically down the middle of the chart and write both your names at the top. Each of you will use half the chart. Each day you can begin by writing down some fact about yourself and then having the learner do the same. For example, write down your favorite vacation spot and describe it, and then ask the learner to do the same. Some other possible topics for conversation could include: a good movie, a pet, a favorite meal, the best part of your last job, or a hope for the future. Learners will be much more relaxed about speaking up during the training if they know something about the person training them and have shared information about themselves.

Principle 2: Adults Want to Be Involved in Their Own Learning

To keep learners involved, you can have them describe what they are doing on the job now and solicit their suggestions for improving the process. They can also participate by reading or writing. A learner's manual, job aid, or handout can save the day. It doesn't have to be elaborate. Six or seven sheets of paper stapled together can involve the learner. Some fill-in-the-blank areas or blank spaces for mind-maps or flow charts encourage writing. Learners who read and write about the topic become focused on the process.

Learners can also participate via directed thinking. Ask a learner to answer questions from question cards; direct his or her attention to the schedule for the day; pose "What if?" or "Why?" questions.

Active learning is another way for learners to become involved. Listening to a lecture is passive. Engaging in a dialogue is active. As much as possible, ask non-threatening, open-ended questions about the material being learned so that the trainee does not mentally leave the room.

Principle 3: What Adults Are Taught Must Be Perceived As Useful

Adults expect what they are learning to be practical and relevant. The following statements apply to this principle:

✓ What adults learn and use immediately will be retained best; and

✓ Immediate use satisfies adults' "need to know."

If you are training new hires, they probably know that what they are learning is necessary for them to keep the new job, but you can extend usefulness further. For example, if you show a trainee a flow chart of the organization, make it an opportunity to show where the job he or she is learning fits into the picture. Stress its importance, and give the learner a sense of the relevance of the task.

Much of what is taught in one-on-one settings can be used immediately, but if there is going to be some lag time, be sure to include extra practice sessions. These can range from operating a piece of equipment at a safe and non-intrusive time, to role playing customer-service skills (with you as the customer on the other end of the line), to actually completing paperwork via a software program. Repeated practice is important for incorporating learning.

> ### Bonus Technique
>
> Watch for those with a high "need to know." You may feel you have thoroughly explained something, only to run into a trainee who asks many questions. This does not necessarily mean that you didn't explain well, nor that the person doesn't get it; it may mean that this learner has a high need for additional information. Have some in-depth printed material available for cases such as these.

Principle 4: Adult Learning Must Be Reinforced

In order to reinforce learning, remember the following suggestions:

1. Build in opportunities for the trainee to receive feedback.

2. Offer feedback that is positive, specific, and constructive.

3. Provide time for practice.

4. Don't assume that learning has taken place.

Creative Training Techniques' Senior Consultant Michele Deck recommends that feedback be of the "sandwich" variety: Sandwich an area for improvement between two areas of positive reinforcement, for example, "I commend you for . . .; I recommend that you . . .; and I commend you for . . . ." That's the formula. Remember that three or four things are about all a person can work on improving at a time, so give the learner your feedback and have him or her master your "recommend" areas before you give your next feedback.

Praise what's right and calmly point out mistakes, being very specific and constructive. The person may have been trained by someone who wildly shouted, "That's wrong!" You will be a welcome relief with your specific instructions.

Build in comprehension benchmarks. Quick fill-in-the-blanks, question cards such as those provided in this book, ten or twelve multiple-choice questions, flow charts, or mind-maps—all these and more can help you test an adult's learning level.

Whether you are training in a classroom or on the job, some thought to the construction of the training process will be helpful. It will remind you when to build in those learning checks and when to include some review activities. This all falls under the topic of training design, the next chapter of this section.

CHAPTER 2

An Eight-Step Process for Designing Training

Have you ever received a backstage pass? Is there a performer you'd really like to meet in person? Dave Arch (1997), in his book *Showmanship for Presenters,* poses the question of just why a person might covet a backstage pass. Certainly one of the top reasons is innate curiosity. Plus, we enjoy looking "behind the scenes." We're interested in how things really work.

Welcome backstage! As the curtain is pulled away in the next few pages, you will discover what goes into the design of an effective one-on-one training program. You will learn an eight-step process that, when properly applied, ensures that no detail will be missed. If you follow this eight-step process each time you're designing any type of training, whether one-on-one or not, you will not be blindsided by the evaluations you receive, and your scores from both trainees and superiors will be higher as they recognize your thoughtful approach to training design.

You will also learn a simple process to measure the results and evaluate how much learning took place. This system will enable you to demonstrate to management that training does indeed make a difference—thereby increasing your own job security! So let's not waste time. Let's begin.

Step 1: List Trainee Needs

Trainers in a corporate or association environment find themselves in a precarious position. Bob Pike (1994), in *The Creative Training Techniques Handbook,* likens it to training while standing on a three-legged stool—balancing in an effort to please up to three different evaluators: the "sender," the "payer," and the "trainee."

The Sender

First, the trainer seeks to please the "sender," the manager of the person who is coming to training. The sender has an agenda as to what should be accomplished through training. Unless the trainer specifically asks, senders typically will not volunteer that information until after the training—and then may criticize the training for not meeting the trainee's needs. Therefore, before beginning to design any one-on-one training, inquire as to what trainee needs are uppermost in the mind of the sender. The Effectiveness Grid that follows is an excellent tool for finding out.

To use the grid, list on the grid the training needs you believe are important for the particular trainee, leaving some blanks for the *sender* to fill in. Ask the sender to circle the number to the right of each blank to indicate the priority he or she assigns to it, with "1" indicating a low priority and "10" a high priority.

Effectiveness Grid

Skill or Knowledge Needed	1	2	3	4	5	6	7	8	9	10
_____	·	·	·	·	·	·	·	·	·	·
_____	·	·	·	·	·	·	·	·	·	·
_____	·	·	·	·	·	·	·	·	·	·
_____	·	·	·	·	·	·	·	·	·	·
_____	·	·	·	·	·	·	·	·	·	·
_____	·	·	·	·	·	·	·	·	·	·
_____	·	·	·	·	·	·	·	·	·	·
_____	·	·	·	·	·	·	·	·	·	·
_____	·	·	·	·	·	·	·	·	·	·
_____	·	·	·	·	·	·	·	·	·	·
_____	·	·	·	·	·	·	·	·	·	·
_____	·	·	·	·	·	·	·	·	·	·
_____	·	·	·	·	·	·	·	·	·	·
_____	·	·	·	·	·	·	·	·	·	·
_____	·	·	·	·	·	·	·	·	·	·
_____	·	·	·	·	·	·	·	·	·	·

The Payer

Also use the Effectiveness Grid to gather input from the *payer,* who may not be the same person as the sender. Depending on organizational structure, monies for the training might be coming from a completely different sector, so make sure that the payer is involved in determining needs and setting goals prior to designing the training. In some cases, the payer could be your own boss, the training manager.

The Trainee

The final leg of the stool represents the *trainee.* Give a copy of the Effectiveness Grid to the trainee to fill out prior to designing the training to gain a better sense of the trainee's own "felt needs" and their order of priority. Of course, the trainee may not be aware of all training needs, as he or she may not have prior experience on a particular new job.

Now compile the information from the sender, the payer, and the trainee, listing the needs by priority, both in general and specifically. In order to avoid an unpleasant surprise later in the process, obtain buy-in on the final list from at least the sender and the payer.

This is also the time to clarify the process for evaluating results as well. Discuss with the sender and payer the method(s) that will be used. Some possibilities include using a pre-test and post-test, interviewing the senders and/or trainees after thirty or more days, or using peer review. If you don't reach an agreement on the desired results and how they will be evaluated, your training could actually meet the trainee's needs, but you would not be able to prove to either party that it had done so.

In the second step of the training design process, you will use a modification of the same Effectiveness Grid to assess the trainee.

Step 2: Assess Your Audience

Have you ever been told a joke, but you just didn't "get it"? Quite possibly the speaker assumed that you had the necessary background information to appreciate the humor. If you are not careful, you can do that to your trainees too. You must take the time to assess the following two areas carefully: prior knowledge and interest in the topic.

Prior Knowledge

If you underestimate what trainees already know about a topic, you will bore them to tears. If you overestimate what trainees know about the topic, you will frustrate them needlessly. Either approach leads to an ineffective training session and to predictably low evaluations.

Let's return to the Effectiveness Grid we used previously and adapt it for use with assessing the trainee as well.

Effectiveness Grid

Skill or Knowledge Needed	1	2	3	4	5	6	7	8	9	10
_____	.	.	.	.	.	.	.	.	.	.
_____	.	.	.	.	.	.	.	.	.	.
_____	.	.	.	.	.	.	.	.	.	.
_____	.	.	.	.	.	.	.	.	.	.
_____	.	.	.	.	.	.	.	.	.	.
_____	.	.	.	.	.	.	.	.	.	.
_____	.	.	.	.	.	.	.	.	.	.
_____	.	.	.	.	.	.	.	.	.	.
_____	.	.	.	.	.	.	.	.	.	.
_____	.	.	.	.	.	.	.	.	.	.
_____	.	.	.	.	.	.	.	.	.	.
_____	.	.	.	.	.	.	.	.	.	.
_____	.	.	.	.	.	.	.	.	.	.
_____	.	.	.	.	.	.	.	.	.	.
_____	.	.	.	.	.	.	.	.	.	.

3 Greatest _____   3 Greatest_____

1._____   1. _____

2._____   2. _____

3._____   3. _____

With the exception of the two lists at the bottom of the page, this grid is identical to the one you used to determine trainee needs earlier. However, this time you will list specific topics that you plan to cover during the training session on the blanks. Ask the trainee to circle his or her personal level of competency on the various areas, with a "10" representing a strong competency and a "1" a low competency. Then ask the trainee to list his or her three *greatest needs* and three *greatest strengths* at the bottom of the page.

Collecting this information ahead of time will not necessarily tell you exactly what the trainee knows about the topics being covered, but it will provide a good indication of what he or she thinks is known. This information also alerts you to the "teachability" of the person. If the data show someone who feels he or she already knows it all, prepare for resistance to even attending your training course.

If the training content lends itself to being tested factually, then an excellent way to evaluate what the trainee knows is to give a test of the material prior to training. By giving a pre-test and then giving the post-test following the training, you will have a quantitative measurement of the program's results.

There is another critical application of a pre-test. Bob Pike and Dave Arch (1997) address the indispensable role of the pre-test in allowing people to test out of the training. The authors believe that many difficult participants would be removed from training rooms across the world if more companies allowed participants to test out of training courses based on pre-test scores. For an excellent book on designing both pre-tests and post-tests, consider Sandra Merwin's book entitled *Evaluation* (1994).

If the material does not lend itself readily to pre-testing by a trainee, you can use the Effectiveness Grid in yet another way for obtaining quantitative data from them. (See Step 3 below.) However, first let's look at how to assess a trainee's interest in the topic prior to the beginning of training.

Interest in the Topic

It is important to know how interested the trainee is in the topic being covered. Is the person going through the training program only because it's a company requirement? Is the person attending with an interest in becoming the best he or she can be? The trainee's level of interest affects how you will deliver the material. Typically, the less interested trainees are in the material, the less motivated they will be and the more involving the presentation must be.

Although you could use a questionnaire to measure someone's interest in a topic, you will typically know the trainee's level of interest from a subjective "gut feeling," just from being around the person. Maslow's hierarchy, shown in Figure 1, can help you here.

First, ask yourself at what motivation level the trainee typically functions. If the person is predominately concerned about food, clothing, and shelter, you will waste energy trying to motivate him or her to "be all that you can be" (self-actualization). Similarly, if "belonging" is a key focus of the trainee, the opportunity to network with both you and others will be indispensable for achieving maximum satisfaction from the training.

Motivating the unmotivated is a topic for an entire book in itself. However, the following two ideas might be useful:

Focus on Long-Range Goals   Whenever possible, make each lesson a part of a whole process, possibly leading to certification. This will increase the trainee's motivation to continue as he or she moves toward an even greater goal.

Focus on Benefits   Scrutinize the course from the perspective of a trainee—analyzing the benefits to the person in both his or her career and personal life. Then emphasize those benefits prior to the training, through your title and subtitle for the course and in how you design the materials. Emphasize the benefits throughout the course itself.

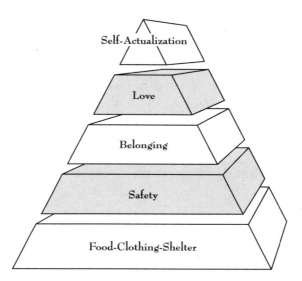

Figure 1.   Maslow's Hierarchy of Needs
From Abraham Maslow, *Motivation and Personality,* Harper and Row, 1954.

Trainees are motivated to learn the most when there's a clear answer to the question: "What's in it for me(WII-FM)?" They have already started to wonder, so it's your job to give the answer.

Step 3: Decide Your Aim

After examining the data you obtained during Steps 1 and 2, during which you determined training needs and assessed your trainee's interest (motivation) and prior knowledge (skills), you are ready to write some objective(s) for the training sessions.

Objectives should *not* be statements about the process itself. State objectives in a way that clearly gives the desired *results* of the learning experience, which are determined by the gap between where the trainee is now and where you (the trainer), the sender, and the payer desire the person to be. Statements of objectives must answer the question: "What are the desired outcomes from this learning experience?" Typically, learning objectives will reflect these desired outcomes in one of three categories: knowing, feeling, and doing.

Knowing

Ask yourself: "What do I want the person to know as a result of taking this training?" This can usually be determined through combining what you learned from giving a pre-test on the material and what you heard the sender and the payer say they expect. Whether the desired knowledge was actually gained during training can be tested by having trainees take a post-test on the same content. Objectives that state what the trainee will *know* are typically the easiest to define and to measure.

Feeling

The next question to ask is: "How do I want the learner to feel as a result of taking this training?" Although it is not quite as easy to measure feelings as it is to measure knowledge, you can use written evaluations and/or interviews, which will be subjective, of course. But feelings are very important, and they must not be overlooked. To quote Bob Pike: "The purpose of training is for trainees to leave impressed with themselves, not intimidated by the trainer. They should leave excited about what they now know that they didn't know before—excited about what they can now do that they couldn't do before and with more confidence about using their new knowledge and skills on the job."

As an example, imagine for a moment that you are training on-line operators for a telemarketing firm. You have established knowledge goals in relation to both product knowledge and the order-taking process itself. You have established performance goals in relation to the successful execution of the order-taking process. But you have failed to include feeling objectives. Many trainees have been very successful in mastering the content and process, but are still leaving the company shortly after completing your training program. It could be that a failure to identify feeling objectives contributed to the high rate of attrition. Because no one paid attention to how the trainees felt about themselves as they performed the job, they learned the skills required of the job itself, but did not feel confident, enthusiastic, and motivated. You could have incorporated activities that contributed toward their feeling good about themselves on the job. The high attrition rate undoubtedly points to a lack of attention to feeling objectives during the planning process.

Doing

The question you must ask in the "doing" category is: "What do I want my trainee to be able to do as a result of taking this course?" A set of behaviorally based objectives provides the best answer for this question.

Behavioral objectives can typically be evaluated through testing or observation during the training session and/or observation back on the job following the training, usually in thirty to sixty days.

After writing each *doing* objective, check to see whether it is possible to observe someone accomplishing the objective. If the answer to that question is "yes," then follow up by deciding how to make the observation. If you cannot think of a way to observe the trainee demonstrating what was learned, rewrite the objective itself until it can be both observed and measured.

Your choice of words is very important when writing measurable objectives. Avoid words such as "comprehend," "understand," "appreciate," or "become aware of," which can neither be observed nor measured. Use action words such as "describe," "discuss," "identify," "define," "demonstrate," and "perform" so that you (and others) will be able to observe and measure a trainee's grasp of each objective.

Be cautious on two points when writing objectives:

1. The objective must be realistic; that is, based on your assessment of the audience (Step 2), can the trainee be reasonably expected to achieve the objectives? If the objectives are not realistic, you are setting yourself up for failure, and learners are sure to experience frustration and discouragement;

2. Next, you must assess whether the completed list of objectives reflects the needs of all parties (the sender, the payer, and the trainee). As a child bears resemblance to the parents, these objectives must carry the stamp of the people who listed them to begin with.

Use a modification of the Effectiveness Grid to incorporate the objectives of knowing, feeling, and doing. Lay out the sheet like the following example, with blanks in the middle and rating scales from 1 to 10 on either side. Print the learning objectives (competencies) on the blanks.

Effectiveness Grid

1 2 3 4 5 6 7 8 9 10

1 2 3 4 5 6 7 8 9 10

. . . .   _____   . . . .

. . . .   _____   . . . .

. . . .   _____   . . . .

. . . .   _____   . . . .

. . . .   _____   . . . .

. . . .   _____   . . . .

. . . .   _____   . . . .

. . . .   _____   . . . .

. . . .   _____   . . . .

. . . .   _____   . . . .

. . . .   _____   . . . .

. . . .   _____   . . . .

. . . .   _____   . . . .

. . . .   _____   . . . .

Use the modified grid as both a pre-training self-evaluation and a post-training self-evaluation for each trainee. Ask the trainee where he or she is in relation to each stated competency at the beginning of the course and again following the course. Use the same grid for senders and payers to obtain even more data to evaluate the success of the training. The results should provide quantitative data to help justify both your role and the validity of the course.

Now that you have determined the goals and objectives of the course, assessed the trainee's motivation, and decided how you will measure the results, it's time to plan the actual course content.

Step 4: Plan Your Approach

Imagine for a moment that you are watching your favorite late-night talk show. The announcer has just introduced the host, and he walks out from backstage. The audience claps feverishly. As the applause subsides, the host begins with these comments: "Tonight my first guest is a favorite of movie-goers the world over. Please join me in welcoming Tom Hanks!" Something screams inside you! "Wait! Wait! I'm not ready for a guest yet!" And indeed, the rest of the audience would probably agree with you. Fortunately, you will never see a talk show begin so abruptly. There is a monologue during which the host bonds with the audience and makes the audience members feel comfortable. These important moments serve as a bridge from where the audience is to where the host wants it to be in preparation for the first guest.

You must also give adequate thought to the beginning of the session. You cannot bombard the trainee with content right from the beginning. Just like those audience members in our imaginary late-night scenario, the learners scream inside "Wait! Wait! I'm not ready yet!" The damage goes far beyond an aesthetically displeasing beginning. The content you present in those initial moments (before the trainees are ready) is wasted. Trainee retention of those pieces of content will be negligible.

One-on-one training is no exception. There must be a planned opening that serves as a bridge to the main content. Here are some ideas for effectively opening the session in a one-on-one setting.

Tell a Story

It's helpful for the trainee to get to know you better in these opening moments. A personal content-related anecdote can help make that connection. Possibly, you have a story about an event that occurred when you took the training you're now delivering. Maybe it's a story of a more general nature of something that happened to you on the way to work. The goal during these opening moments is for the trainee to identify with you. Stories that the person can relate to help to achieve this goal. We often refer to the content of these opening moments as "small talk." However, their importance is anything but small.

Ask a Question

Any type of a question forces the mind to respond. For example, what if someone said: "Now whatever you do, don't think of the answer to the following question: 'What is 4 + 4?' Now remember *not* to think of the answer." It's nearly impossible isn't it? Try another one: "Remember, do not think of the answer, but 'What is 2 x 3?'" Did you think of the answer again? Of course you did! That's the power of questions. Our minds crave closure. Questions are just too open-ended!

Here's a structure for a question that works particularly well in opening situations. "Have you noticed that . . . ?" Fill in the blank with some content-related subject (for example, "that people are stressed when learning new computer programs?" "that many trainers go too fast in their training?" etc.) Such a question does not require a lengthy response, which might make the trainee uncomfortable. It requires only a polite nod of the head or a smile, but it helps to break the ice.

Make a Promise

In the basic Creative Training Techniques™ two-day seminar, presenters typically promise participants that they will receive over one hundred training techniques by the end of the second day. Some people predictably start to count. At the end of the first day, many of the trainers make a list to see how close they are to fulfilling their initial promise. They not only make a promise, but also demonstrate that they take that promise seriously. Promises engage people. What benefits could you promise a trainee at the beginning of the training that would help to put that person on the same track with you right from the start?

Start Them Laughing

Dave Arch (1997) devotes an entire chapter in his book, *Showmanship for Presenters,* to helping the trainer find his or her own style of humor. Arch recommends finding out what we do or say outside of the training room in our daily encounters with other people that tends to make them laugh. The answer holds the clues to our own singular styles of humor.

The most successful type of humor is that which makes the participant and the trainer laugh together about what might happen during the training or about a personal anecdote that either might share. Laughing breaks down barriers and opens our minds to new experiences and information. It is a stress reliever and a very helpful tool in increasing the trainee's "teachability" and ability to retain what you teach in the training room.

Share Your Credentials

Probably no one will introduce you formally to the trainee. However, for maximum trainee receptivity to the lessons you are teaching, it is important to share your credentials at the beginning. Give evidence of your qualifications to teach the course and why the person should listen to you. Quite often this information can be shared anecdotally (for example, "When I took this same training in 1985 . . . ," "I had a professor in my master's program who always said . . . ," "Congratulations! You are the seventy-fifth person I've trained on this system!")

No matter how you complete those sentences—based on your own credentials—be sure that it relates to benefits for the learner. If you have taught seventy-four people this same material, the trainee will have a tendency to relax, assuming that everything that can go wrong has gone wrong already. If you have just completed a master's program, the trainee is assured of learning the very latest in the field. And so on.

Make a Profound Statement

Try making this "profound" statement: "There are five reasons why someone should be fired from this company immediately!" Now there may not really be five reasons, but be assured that you have captured the listener's attention right from the beginning.

Cite an Unusual Statistic

Companies are full of interesting data. Find out how many customers have been serviced since the company was founded or how many people have gone through the very training you are delivering. Trainees are especially interested in how many customers are affected as they execute their jobs. Collect statistics and find uses for them. You might even have the person guess the answer before revealing the statistic. A source for statistics is listed in the Bibliography and Additional Resources at the end of this book.

Use a Visual Aid or Prop

Carry something unusual into the training room on the first day and set it somewhere in the front of the room before beginning. Indicate that the item will be dealt with later and then use it later to emphasize a key point. Another idea is to come into the room on the first day, give the learner a sealed envelope, and ask him or her to keep it. At the end of the training segment, ask for the envelope and open it. Inside could be a slogan that captures the essence of the course or an outline of the content. Unusual props raise curiosity and engage the learner.

As you prepare an opening approach, here are some questions you might ask to evaluate its potential effectiveness for one-on-one training:

✓ Does it break the trainee's preoccupation with other matters and enable him or her to focus on what's happening in the training?

✓ Does it facilitate breaking down barriers and building bridges between you and the trainee?

✓ Is it relevant to the content about to be studied?

✓ Is it fun both for you as the trainer and for the learner?

✓ Does it help raise the curiosity of the learner?

If you can answer "yes" to those five questions, the approach is a winner!

Step 5: Develop a Lesson Plan

Now you are ready to design the lesson itself. There is no faster method than building a mind-map! Mind-maps consist of a series of lines and circles that build on one another to form a visual display of the subject. Figure 2 is a copy of a mind-map used to construct this book.

Notice that the title (main theme) is at the center of the map and that branches come out from that core in all directions. The beauty of mind-mapping is that one's thoughts do not need to be sequential. As each thought triggers another, the process triggers yet another. After you have completed a mind-map of the training content, it is a simple task to organize it into a typical sequential outline with Roman numerals and capital letters.

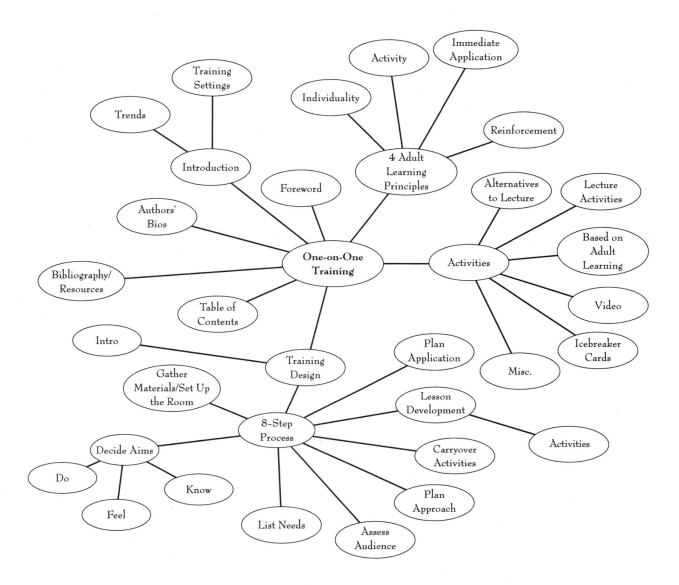

Figure 2.   Sample Mind-Map

Try one right now on a blank sheet of paper—dumping from your mind onto the paper all of your thoughts regarding a course you are currently designing. When your mind-map is complete, you probably will be looking down at a mountain of content. All of it will not be equally important, so next divide it into three categories: "must know," "nice to know," and "where to find." Now you can build the course without overwhelming your trainee.

Put content that is absolutely essential for the trainee to know in the "must know" category. You *must* cover this material as part of the course itself. Typically, the longer a trainer has taught a course, the more he or she thinks belongs here. However, it is wise not to put too much material into this category.

The "nice to know" category consists of material that is not essential to the trainee's performance on the job. This may include shortcuts, skill-polishing techniques, and items that require greater finesse that you have found helpful, but which are not absolutely necessary for the trainee to know.

"Where to find" items are those that the trainee will need to be able to find back on the job but that do not need to be committed to memory. In many training situations, this category will contain the majority of the information. The amount of material might be so massive that it would be futile to train anyone to master it. Train people instead to find the answers when they are needed back on the job. In the Tips and Techniques Section of this book, you will find several ways to encourage trainees to build their own job aids.

When developing your lessons, remember that the attention span of the average adult is about twenty minutes, so plan with this in mind. Break the content into twenty-minute chunks using the mnemonic aid we call CPR, shown in Figure 3. In every twenty-minute segment, (1) introduce content, (2) encourage participation with that content, and (3) review what has been covered previously before adding new information. For maximum effectiveness, never go more than twenty minutes without incorporating some major change in style or content.

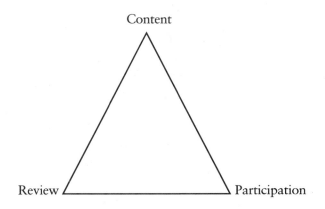

Figure 3.   The CPR Model for Program Design

"Chunking" the content in this manner really makes the time fly for the trainee—and it increases retention too.

Most of us are very adept at covering the content in the CPR model. We are good at introducing new content. However, we tend to forget the amount of processing time needed by the trainee to incorporate something before being able to absorb more content. Consequently, the participation step in the model is crucial. You must allow some processing time at least every twenty minutes so that the trainee can interact with the content you have introduced. Allow time for participation, processing, and review before moving on and introducing new content. In the Tips and Techniques Section of this book you will find many activities designed to help you and your trainee process and review material.

Step 6: Plan Lesson Application

From the title of your course to the cover of your workbook to the content you choose to incorporate, remember to keep the entire course benefit-based. The trainee is always asking: "So what?" He or she really wants to find meaning and to have the content be made personal. Trainees wonder: "What's in it for me?" "Will it make my job easier?" "Will it position me for a promotion?" "Does it have any carryover benefits to my personal life?"

Because the average employee changes jobs seven times in his or her lifetime, this last question is becoming increasingly important. We must look at how our training will help employees, not only in a current position but throughout their careers.

Seeing the benefits can really build trainee motivation for taking the course, especially if you find a way to build benefits into the pre-training publicity!

As you reflect back on your course goals, make sure that the skills you are teaching can be easily applied back on the job. Rather than assuming that trainees will make connections to applications themselves, utilize concrete real-world examples of how others have taken the information they have learned from you and made a difference.

Once again, the best way to proceed is not to tell trainees how to apply the material, but to *have them tell you* what they plan to do differently back on the job as a result of the training. Have the learner declare how he or she will apply what is being learned at many points throughout the course, and you will have integrated this important step seamlessly into your presentation.

The natural next step is planning for carryover.

Step 7: Plan a Carryover Activity

Now you must find strategies to accomplish what the training experts call "training transfer." To do this, you need some techniques that take the content out of the training room and back to the job site. You need to set up a process to check on the results of training over the next thirty, sixty, and even ninety days.

Certainly, one of the easier ways is to observe the trainee back on the job and to interview the sender thirty days later and then to follow up with any remedial training. However, you could also ask the trainee to make a list of personal goals for implementing changes back on the job and mail the list to him or her in thirty days to serve as a reminder.

Another idea is to use a small icon that serves as a reminder of the desired change in behavior and ask the trainee to carry that piece at all times for the next thirty days. Every time the person sees the icon, he or she is reminded of the desired behavioral change. You can even make it more interesting by requiring the trainee to produce the icon when asked any time during the next thirty days.

Other ways to remind trainees include moving a watch to the opposite wrist or wearing a tag of some kind on the clothing for thirty days as a reminder of the desired behavioral change.

The method you use to remind the trainee of content is not as important as the fact that there is some kind of reminder.

Step 8: Gather Material and Prepare the Room

Pulling together materials for your training is the final step in the training-design process. Be sure to allocate enough time for this stage or you may not have time when the trainee arrives to break the ice and set the tone for the session. This would be very unfortunate.

As you set the scene for the first session, have some music playing to help fill the silence and overcome any initial awkwardness. Select a style of music that communicates the desired mood for the training—laid back, high energy, or just plain fun. The music should help set the expectations of the trainee from the first moment. Check the temperature in the room. A room too cold or too warm can have a direct relationship on the level of content retention.

Be ready to sit down and make some small talk to establish rapport, which is critical to the success of the training session. Set your chair and the trainee's chair so that nothing is between them. The arrangement must communicate a sense of your approachability and vulnerability. Anything between the two of you will communicate that you do not trust the person and are not willing to be vulnerable.

As a consideration to the person you are training, give directions to the bathroom or other facilities, if needed, and present an agenda for the training. This will ease the trainee's mind and enable him or her to concentrate on the training.

Finally, have some food available. There's nothing quite like food to break down walls and help people relate to one another. There's nothing like a supply of cold drinking water to help keep both trainee and trainer alert throughout the training session.

As you start the session, use the plan you developed in Step 4 and begin bridging to your content. Because of your attention to details in these planning stages, you can now relax and enjoy that dynamic process referred to as training.

Whether you are training someone in a separate room or on the job, using these eight steps to plan the process will be immensely helpful for you. Especially remember to use the CPR model to build in some learning checks and to include some review activities. Make full use of the learning techniques in the next section.

Good luck to you as you engage the learner!

Section 2

TIPS AND TECHNIQUES FOR ONE-ON-ONE TRAINING

Some of the tips and techniques that follow may seem simple and commonly known, but they have been collected here for the benefit of the reader who will become a trainer, perhaps a manager or peer who is to engage in one-on-one training for the first time.

Tips for Incorporating Techniques

If you are used to classroom training and know the value of interaction among participants, moving to one-on-one training can be frustrating. You need some training techniques that will spark the same level of interest, result in retention of the content, and yet fit your one-on-one situation. We have provided them in this section of the book. Each technique is accompanied by an illustration that lists the goals likely to be met by using the technique. The items listed are taken directly from the principles of adult learning and from the needs of the typical one-on-one training environment. The illustration looks likes this:

- ☐ Revisit Content
- ☐ Promote Safety
- ☐ Honor Values
- ☐ Give Control
- ☐ Encourage Directed Thinking
- ☐ Encourage Active Listening
- ☐ Give Positive Feedback
- ☐ Promote Reading, Writing, or Speaking

Different techniques are designed for different purposes. The illustration has been designed to make it easy for you to see which are suitable for your needs. The check marks indicate the uses for each one. Select those that best meet the needs of your learner and will help him or her transfer learning.

It is also important for you to use many different techniques to keep the learner interested and involved in his or her own learning. Some sessions will be short, others longer, but use what seems appropriate at the time. Remember that the goal is to enhance the learner's experience.

Tips When You Have to Lecture

Even with attention to detail and pre-planning, there are times when you just have to deliver at least a mini-lecture. When those times roll around, remember the following tips:

1. Train in twenty-minute chunks. Each twenty-minute segment should end with some interaction between you and the trainee or some physical activity, such as operating a piece of equipment.

2. Divide content into six-point groupings. Six points is enough for a twenty-minute segment.

3. Begin each mini-lecture with an overview. Introduce the major points that will be given.

4. Use visual images to explain the content and to stimulate the learner's imagination. Visuals also promote whole-brain learning, which enhances retention.

5. Use analogies. Tell a "story" or give examples. Avoid jargon. Keep your language simple and straightforward.

6. Provide periodic summaries. Remember that content must be revisited six times for full retention.

7. Incorporate feedback consistently. Feedback opportunities give the learner a chance to revisit the content and also see how he or she is doing.

Incorporate these tips, even when you have to lecture the learner, and the results will be much better.

Tips When You Train with Videos

Videos offer an alternative way to convey information. They constitute a break for you in the delivery of content and refresh the trainee with new voices and a new medium. However, there is an old rule that says: "When the lights go down, the retention goes down." Many suspect a rule could also be: "When the video goes on, the trainee checks out."

Tying a video to a paper-and-pencil task keeps the trainee in the room both physically *and mentally.* If your training involves videos, remember this simple rule: Don't show a video without putting a piece of paper in the learner's hands. That sheet of paper may be a fill-in-the-blank exercise, a simple crossword puzzle, a mini-quiz, a matching quiz, or whatever works for the content.

The trainee will look at the paper while you explain that the information needed to complete the exercise is in the upcoming video. Say, "Watch for it. We'll take a few moments at the end of the video for you to complete the exercise alone; then we'll go over your responses together."

Videos should be shown in approximately twenty-minute time frames, so break longer videos one or more times. At each break, debrief before beginning a new segment. Hand out new sheets of paper with something to fill out about the next segment. Each sheet of paper can accommodate eight to twelve key points.

This method alerts the trainee to upcoming key areas and also provides a four-time visit of content: the preview, the video itself, filling out the paper, and discussing answers with you.

After you have provided a means for keeping the trainee's attention, here are some tips for getting the most out of the video itself:

1. Always preview the video. Never use a video you have not seen. It could be that some of the language used will offend the learner or even that a recommendation is made that you do not support.

2. Preview the video prior to looking at any support materials. Always look at the video with fresh eyes and with the training objective in mind in order to see every way that the video can suit the needs of the trainee without being unduly influenced by suggestions from the creators of the video.

3. Preview the video twice. The first time will give you a sense of the total content of the video so that you can look for what your trainee should watch for. The second time, look for points at which to break the video for discussion or an activity.

4. Be sure the equipment is in running order and that you know how to run it. If you will be using a remote control, make sure that the batteries are working and also learn how to run the machine itself.

5. Cue the video in advance. Many videos have long leaders that can frustrate viewers before they even see any of the content.

6. Use viewing partnerships—you and the trainee. List the specifics each of you will watch for. For example, one of you might look for how one particular person acted or reacted and why. The other might watch from the viewpoint of the other person in the video. When people have something specific to watch for, it makes a video more interesting and challenging.

7. Come up with a set of questions for later discussion. Some possible questions could be: "What was the problem here?" "What caused the problem?" "What should [person in video] do?" "How could this person have handled the situation differently?"

Partial Mind–Maps

- ☑ Revisit Content
- ☐ Promote Safety
- ☑ Honor Values
- ☑ Give Control
- ☑ Encourage Directed Thinking
- ☐ Encourage Active Listening
- ☑ Give Positive Feedback
- ☑ Promote Reading, Writing, or Speaking

The objective of using mind-maps is to have the trainee create a memory-enhancing visual representation of the information being taught. This type of map can be used with all soft skills or with training that involves procedures and sequences.

Give the trainee a partial mind-map at the beginning of the class (or segment). (See the sample map in Chapter 2.) Go over the headings for the mind-map with the trainee, which serves as an overview of the training content and alerts him or her to the various kinds of information that will be covered.

At the end of each appropriate segment of the training, have the trainee enter the details (or the steps in the process or procedure) under the appropriate headings. When the mind-map is complete, the trainee has created his or her own visual aid. Multiple mind-maps can be made and used every day for training that has taken many weeks and covered a variety of topics. They can be used to sum up a three-hour or a one-day class.

TECHNIQUE 2

Build a Notebook

- ☑ Revisit Content
- ☐ Promote Safety
- ☑ Honor Values
- ☑ Give Control
- ☑ Encourage Directed Thinking
- ☐ Encourage Active Listening
- ☐ Give Positive Feedback
- ☑ Promote Reading, Writing, or Speaking

Sometimes a trainee has to learn new information *and* a new memory system, too. In some settings it could be appropriate to ask the trainee: "How would *you* remember this best?" By creating his or her own retrieval system, the trainee can better internalize the information. Keeping a notebook is an excellent technique for tracking everything during long training sessions that provide a large volume of information.

At Kodak, some trainers give each trainee a three-ring binder with alphabetized page dividers. During the training process, each piece of information is processed by the trainee and entered in the notebook in the way that makes the most sense to him or her. Try this technique with your learner.

TECHNIQUE 3

Crossword Puzzles

- ☑ Revisit Content
- ☐ Promote Safety
- ☐ Honor Values
- ☐ Give Control
- ☑ Encourage Directed Thinking
- ☐ Encourage Active Listening
- ☑ Give Positive Feedback
- ☑ Promote Reading, Writing, or Speaking

Michele Deck is a superb trainer and a pioneer in the use of interactive training activities. Michele suggests that using crossword puzzles is a natural way to review activities in a one-on-one setting, as they engage the learner actively in recalling the lesson. You have great flexibility with puzzles, as they can be easily developed. See the Bibliography and Additional Resources for software that makes it easy to prepare one quickly with up to fifty words and definitions, or try *www.crosswords.com.*

One or more puzzles can be used to enliven otherwise dull content. If you plan to use a puzzle for review at the end of a three-hour class, for example, you might want to introduce the puzzle at the beginning of the class. This serves to preview the content for the trainee and alerts him or her to key segments of the upcoming training.

Create a File

- ✓ Revisit Content
- ✓ Promote Safety
- ☐ Honor Values
- ✓ Give Control
- ✓ Encourage Directed Thinking
- ☐ Encourage Active Listening
- ✓ Give Positive Feedback
- ✓ Promote Reading, Writing, or Speaking

At the beginning of the session, bring a file box containing laminated 3" x 5" cards on which you have written questions that the trainee must know how to answer before the end of the training. These cards can be categorized according to the content; alphabetized; color-coded by type of information, by function, or by process; or whatever. The content will drive the division. Give the trainee an empty file box containing appropriate dividers.

At the end of each day, at the end of a training segment, or whenever it is appropriate, sit down together and ask questions that the trainee should be able to answer at this point, pulling cards from the file, one at a time. If the trainee can answer the question, the card goes into his or her file box. If the trainee cannot answer the question, keep the card.

The goal, of course, is for the trainee to have all the cards in his or her file box at the end of the training and be able to keep the file box as a job aid.

This technique provides for thorough revisits of content, especially if you revisit all of the questions one more time at the very end of the training. That will enable the trainee to review any information that has not been retained.

It is a given that you must praise the trainee for correct answers and provide the answers for any cards that you return to your own file. The trainee must never be made to feel like a failure.

Flow Charts for Previewing

- ☑ Revisit Content
- ☑ Promote Safety
- ☐ Honor Values
- ☑ Give Control
- ☑ Encourage Directed Thinking
- ☑ Encourage Active Listening
- ☐ Give Positive Feedback
- ☐ Promote Reading, Writing, or Speaking

If your topic lends itself to flow charts, cut out pieces of paper to represent the steps in the system you will be training someone about. Literally walk the trainee through the steps and procedures as you lay them on the floor prior to training.

This technique allows the trainee to gain a grasp of what is to come during the training and helps him or her actually see how everything fits together. This is especially useful for visual learners.

Flow Charts for Ongoing Training

- [✓] Revisit Content
- [✓] Promote Safety
- [ ] Honor Values
- [ ] Give Control
- [✓] Encourage Directed Thinking
- [✓] Encourage Active Listening
- [ ] Give Positive Feedback
- [ ] Promote Reading, Writing, or Speaking

Prepare the steps in a process being learned ahead of time on color-coded paper. Have the trainee lay out the entire process on the floor or on a large table. If you use the floor, you can ask the trainee to stand on each piece of paper and move from step to step, describing and discussing the components with you.

Alternatively, you could stand on the pieces of paper yourself and ask the trainee to guide you through the process as you move from one to the next or use a pointer or marker.

Use the process at the beginning, when you would naturally not expect the trainee to be familiar with the process, and several times during the training.

TECHNIQUE 7

See One, Do One, Teach One

✓	Revisit Content
☐	Promote Safety
✓	Honor Values
✓	Give Control
✓	Encourage Directed Thinking
☐	Encourage Active Listening
✓	Give Positive Feedback
☐	Promote Reading, Writing, or Speaking

George Stanley of Hewlett-Packard first introduced us to what seems to be the training byword for HP: "See one, do one, teach one." And a great concept it is. This is more than a technique; it is an entire training approach. You can use it when teaching a skill on a piece of equipment or when teaching a specific task, such as "operate the forklift safely."

First show the learner how to do the task correctly ("See one"). This may take more than one demonstration. As you explain the process, include opportunities for the learner to ask questions. Decide in conjunction with the learner whether he or she is ready to attempt the task ("Do one). This second step might have to be repeated many times, and the demonstration step may have to be repeated.

When you and the learner agree that the learner is ready, move to Step 3, "Teach one." You must stay in role as the trainee during the entire teach-one phase. No fair jumping in to correct or take over. Many trainers ask a peer to come in to serve as "the student," while they disappear. This method takes some of the pressure off so that the trainee can show that the information or skill has been mastered.

The Effectiveness Grid

- ☑ Revisit Content
- ☐ Promote Safety
- ☐ Honor Values
- ☐ Give Control
- ☐ Encourage Directed Thinking
- ☐ Encourage Active Listening
- ☑ Give Positive Feedback
- ☑ Promote Reading, Writing, or Speaking

Make up an Effectiveness Grid listing the skills to be learned. (See the sample on the following page.) Have the trainee rank himself or herself on knowledge of the skill prior to the training. Besides giving you the opportunity to find out what the trainee knows, using an Effectiveness Grid also provides a preview of the training content for the trainee.

The grid can be used throughout the training by having the trainee fill it out with different colors of ink at different times to track his or her progress.

This technique allows you to acknowledge prior learning (the first principle of adult learning) and reinforces what was learned (the fourth principle). It becomes an ongoing way to revisit content. The grid is also an effective tool to use at the beginning and end of longer training sessions, but only for programs whose contents can be listed on one grid. It is better to use one grid for each segment of content.

Effectiveness Grid

Skill or Knowledge Needed	1	2	3	4	5	6	7	8	9	10
_____	·	·	·	·	·	·	·	·	·	·
_____	·	·	·	·	·	·	·	·	·	·
_____	·	·	·	·	·	·	·	·	·	·
_____	·	·	·	·	·	·	·	·	·	·
_____	·	·	·	·	·	·	·	·	·	·
_____	·	·	·	·	·	·	·	·	·	·
_____	·	·	·	·	·	·	·	·	·	·
_____	·	·	·	·	·	·	·	·	·	·
_____	·	·	·	·	·	·	·	·	·	·
_____	·	·	·	·	·	·	·	·	·	·
_____	·	·	·	·	·	·	·	·	·	·
_____	·	·	·	·	·	·	·	·	·	·
_____	·	·	·	·	·	·	·	·	·	·
_____	·	·	·	·	·	·	·	·	·	·
_____	·	·	·	·	·	·	·	·	·	·
_____	·	·	·	·	·	·	·	·	·	·

TECHNIQUE 9

The Toast

☐ Revisit Content
☑ Promote Safety
☑ Honor Values
☐ Give Control
☐ Encourage Directed Thinking
☑ Encourage Active Listening
☑ Give Positive Feedback
☐ Promote Reading,
   Writing, or Speaking

We know how effective a celebratory close is in a formal classroom. After all, a powerful close is a terrific memory enhancer. Creative Training Techniques Senior Consultant Lori Backer recommends that a sense of celebration also be built into one-on-one training by filling beautiful glasses or mugs with fruit punch, apple cider, or Kool Aid®, and at the end of the training "toasting" each other as a celebration of learning that has taken place.

Let the trainee keep the glass or mug. In fact, if your budget allows and there are many people being trained, purchase custom mugs for this ritual with the sequence of steps, key points, or whatever information would be most helpful for the trainee to remember printed on the mug.

TECHNIQUE 10

Daily Checklist

- ☑ Revisit Content
- ☑ Promote Safety
- ☐ Honor Values
- ☑ Give Control
- ☑ Encourage Directed Thinking
- ☑ Encourage Active Listening
- ☑ Give Positive Feedback
- ☑ Promote Reading, Writing, or Speaking

It is useful to begin each training day by going over a "Daily Checklist" to preview the day for the trainee. This technique has the following benefits:

✓ It involves active listening.

✓ It clarifies the goals for the day; and

✓ It becomes a guide to measure the trainee's progress.

Revisit the list prior to lunch, at the afternoon break, and again at the close of the day.

This technique is a wonderful memory enhancer, while providing a safe learning environment for the trainee by using a good structure and listing clear goals.

Scrabble® Review

- ☑ Revisit Content
- ☐ Promote Safety
- ☐ Honor Values
- ☑ Give Control
- ☑ Encourage Directed Thinking
- ☐ Encourage Active Listening
- ☐ Give Positive Feedback
- ☑ Promote Reading, Writing, or Speaking

You need a small box and a set of Scrabble® tiles. Remove most of the vowels from the tile set. At the close of a segment of information, have the trainee draw out an appropriate number of tiles and come up with one sentence for each tile drawn that serves to review the content. Each review sentence should begin with a word that has the same letter as one of the tiles.

Scrabble tiles are also available with words on them.

Move the Dot

☑	Revisit Content
☐	Promote Safety
☑	Honor Values
☐	Give Control
☑	Encourage Directed Thinking
☑	Encourage Active Listening
☑	Give Positive Feedback
☐	Promote Reading, Writing, or Speaking

Creative Training Techniques Senior Consultant Michele Deck gives us this wonderful technique for training on specific skills. When a skill set is introduced, have the trainee take a small, colored dot and place the dot on the face of his or her watch. (If the trainee does not wear a watch, provide an inexpensive watch that can be used during the training and taken home as a training reminder.)

Once the trainee has demonstrated competency in that skill, give him or her a name tag. Remove the dot from the watch and put it on the name tag. Then introduce the next new skill being taught, along with a dot of another color and follow the same process.

In training that involves the mastery of many skills, the colorful name tag is a testimony to the learning that is going on. This is a powerful motivation technique.

Chances Are

- ☑ Revisit Content
- ☐ Promote Safety
- ☐ Honor Values
- ☑ Give Control
- ☐ Encourage Directed Thinking
- ☐ Encourage Active Listening
- ☑ Give Positive Feedback
- ☐ Promote Reading, Writing, or Speaking

Another great technique from Lori Backer is to fill an opaque bag, such as a brown lunch sack, with red, green, blue, and white poker chips after designating each color as an indicator of a particular action. For example, red might represent taking an extra ten minutes for a break; blue might indicate that the person can ask any question he or she likes of the other; green might allow the trainee or the trainer to draw a five-point question from a particular stack of question cards (prepared earlier by the trainer) and either answer it or ask it of the other person; and white might indicate that the trainee or trainer can draw a twenty-five-point question from a different stack (also prepared in advance) and answer it or ask it.

Neither the trainer nor the trainee should be able to see the color of the chip he or she is drawing out of the bag. The two draw at the same time, one chip each. They then complete the two activities indicated by the color of the chips they drew.

How often and when the drawing is done depends on the length of the training and the amount of content. For example, in eight-week classes the drawing could be done four times each Friday. In a one-week class, the chips could be drawn once or twice a day. The value assigned to the chips can also be changed periodically.

TECHNIQUE 14

Stump the Trainer

- ☑ Revisit Content
- ☐ Promote Safety
- ☑ Honor Values
- ☑ Give Control
- ☑ Encourage Directed Thinking
- ☑ Encourage Active Listening
- ☑ Give Positive Feedback
- ☐ Promote Reading, Writing, or Speaking

For training that takes more than one day, a nice technique to use is "Stump the Trainer." For policies and procedures or for any content for which a trainee must master a lot of information, it provides an incentive for active learning.

For this technique, a reward system is needed, such as points toward a free lunch or toward a prize. A Tootsie® Roll or some other actual prize is also effective. To play, the trainee must carefully revisit the content of a specific lesson and come up with an agreed on number of questions pertaining to the content. The trainee then asks the trainer the questions, and if he or she can stump the trainer with any of the questions, a prize is awarded.

This technique is highly motivating for the trainee and gives him or her control over the learning.

Who, What, Where, When, Why, and How

☑	Revisit Content
☐	Promote Safety
☐	Honor Values
☐	Give Control
☑	Encourage Directed Thinking
☐	Encourage Active Listening
☐	Give Positive Feedback
☑	Promote Reading, Writing, or Speaking

Doug McCallum reminds us to ask ourselves whether or not our training lends itself to the tried-and-true questions: who, what, where, when, why, and how.

Your trainee may respond well to being asked these questions orally or in writing. Define your content in these terms, then ask the learner to do the same. It may become clear to you exactly what your trainee has learned and what he or she still needs to review.

Doug recommends asking the following questions about every topic:

✓ What would you do next?

✓ Why would you do that?

✓ Who do you know whom you might ask for information?

✓ When would there be a reason to do that?

✓ How will you do that?

✓ Where can you find further resources?

TECHNIQUE 16

Demonstrations

☑	Revisit Content
☐	Promote Safety
☐	Honor Values
☑	Give Control
☑	Encourage Directed Thinking
☐	Encourage Active Listening
☐	Give Positive Feedback
☑	Promote Reading, Writing, or Speaking

"Actions speak louder than words" was never more true than in training. Never talk about a competency when you can demonstrate that competency.

Ask the learner to demonstrate his or her proficiency with a process for you. Sometimes it's fun to come in through the back door—showing knowledge by demonstrating how not to do something, so don't be afraid to have him or her demonstrate how something should *not* be done.

These demonstrations can take place either on the actual job site or under controlled conditions in a training room.

Debates

- ☑ Revisit Content
- ☐ Promote Safety
- ☑ Honor Values
- ☐ Give Control
- ☑ Encourage Directed Thinking
- ☐ Encourage Active Listening
- ☐ Give Positive Feedback
- ☑ Promote Reading, Writing, or Speaking

Debates are a particularly effective technique when an organizational or job change has been proposed or is being undertaken. Learners can debate with you how the new way is better (or worse) than the old way. You can take one position and have the person take the other, then switch. The two of you will find it's not only fun to play the devil's advocate but that it raises important issues of understanding.

Be sure to explain that the learner should not interpret what you say as "right" because of your position as the trainer.

TECHNIQUE 18

Panel Discussions

☑ Revisit Content
☐ Promote Safety
☐ Honor Values
☐ Give Control
☑ Encourage Directed Thinking
☑ Encourage Active Listening
☐ Give Positive Feedback
☐ Promote Reading, Writing, or Speaking

Invite a panel of "experts" (those who are already using the skill) to come to your training session. Hold a roundtable discussion about what they've discovered while actually applying the skills or knowledge you're teaching.

This technique not only makes the learning more fun for your trainee, but it strengthens the skills and knowledge of the panel members too.

Interviews

- [✓] Revisit Content
- [ ] Promote Safety
- [ ] Honor Values
- [✓] Give Control
- [ ] Encourage Directed Thinking
- [✓] Encourage Active Listening
- [ ] Give Positive Feedback
- [ ] Promote Reading, Writing, or Speaking

Have the trainee prepare a set of interview questions about your topic. Then, instead of holding a panel discussion, bring in one person already using the skills being taught. Have the trainee interview the "expert" as he or she shares knowledge that can only be gained through experience.

This technique can also be used for "soft" skills, such as listening or communicating.

Testimonials

	Revisit Content
✓	Revisit Content
	Promote Safety
✓	Honor Values
	Give Control
	Encourage Directed Thinking
✓	Encourage Active Listening
	Give Positive Feedback
	Promote Reading, Writing, or Speaking

Bring in some people who have already taken your course to increase the trainee's confidence that he or she can learn the skills or knowledge being taught. Spend a whole session discussing such topics as what was most important, what was least important, and what else should be learned.

Obviously, this approach could be combined very effectively with an interview format.

Brainstorming

☐	Revisit Content
☐	Promote Safety
☑	Honor Values
☑	Give Control
☑	Encourage Directed Thinking
☐	Encourage Active Listening
☐	Give Positive Feedback
☑	Promote Reading, Writing, or Speaking

Have the learner practice problem solving by brainstorming all possible options before selecting the most appropriate ones. The most effective way to brainstorm is by withholding evaluation of the idea until later, so you may have to remind the learner to list as many options as possible before determining the feasibility of any of them.

Another great place to use brainstorming is at the beginning of the training session. Have the trainee list what he or she wants to get out the course. Having the person declare his or her own objectives for the course (before you declare yours) strengthens the person's ownership of the material as you go along. Later, have the person return to his or her initial list and identify ways in which the objectives have been met through training.

It may be tempting to add to the person's brainstormed listing, but do this only if crucial points have been left out. Remember not to evaluate the items, but to use them as points of discussion.

TECHNIQUE 22

Field Trips

☑	Revisit Content
☐	Promote Safety
☐	Honor Values
☑	Give Control
☐	Encourage Directed Thinking
☑	Encourage Active Listening
☐	Give Positive Feedback
☑	Promote Reading, Writing, or Speaking

Break up "classroom claustrophobia" by taking the participant on a field trip to an area in which the skill he or she is learning is actually being used. This could be the factory floor or at a vendor or customer site.

Be sure to have the person prepare ahead of time so that he or she will be actively looking for answers to specific questions while observing a process. Have the trainee prepare a checklist so that nothing will be missed.

Projects

☐ Revisit Content
☐ Promote Safety
☑ Honor Values
☑ Give Control
☑ Encourage Directed Thinking
☐ Encourage Active Listening
☑ Give Positive Feedback
☐ Promote Reading,
   Writing, or Speaking

Projects work well for applying and demonstrating knowledge that's been acquired. The project can be a simple, specific assignment (fill out a report, complete a requisition) or a longer undertaking involving actual work on the job. By using either type, you can better assess the person's understanding of the material being learned.

In addition, projects provide a nice change of pace, as the learner typically works independently until ready for the trainer's assessment.

TECHNIQUE 24

Reports

- [ ] Revisit Content
- [ ] Promote Safety
- [x] Honor Values
- [x] Give Control
- [x] Encourage Directed Thinking
- [ ] Encourage Active Listening
- [ ] Give Positive Feedback
- [ ] Promote Reading, Writing, or Speaking

Give a specific assignment to write a report and a deadline for presenting it to you. Suggest some resource material, if needed. The learner may dislike the idea of putting something in writing, but knowledge gained through a little struggle often increases the retention of that knowledge.

The report can serve as a learning aid back on the job and as reading material for future trainees.

Case Studies

- [ ] Revisit Content
- [ ] Promote Safety
- [x] Honor Values
- [x] Give Control
- [x] Encourage Directed Thinking
- [ ] Encourage Active Listening
- [x] Give Positive Feedback
- [x] Promote Reading,
  Writing, or Speaking

Case studies are somewhat like projects. Give the learner information about a specific real-world scenario that is similar to what might be encountered on the job and see how he or she would apply the skills being acquired in your course. This could be done either orally or in writing.

Be sure to give feedback on how your trainee handled the case and discuss any other ways he or she might try to solve the problems illustrated by it.

Role Plays

- [ ] Revisit Content
- [✓] Promote Safety
- [ ] Honor Values
- [✓] Give Control
- [✓] Encourage Directed Thinking
- [✓] Encourage Active Listening
- [✓] Give Positive Feedback
- [ ] Promote Reading, Writing, or Speaking

Role playing is a highly effective way to see how the learner will act back on the job. Use any situations from the actual workplace, or make up situations that use specific skills you are teaching, such as listening or giving feedback. For example, play the role of an irate customer on the telephone as the learner plays the role of the receptionist, and then trade roles.

Because it is only you and one learner, there are no passive observers! Everyone is involved, and there is less nervousness about "performing."

Skits

- ✓ Revisit Content
- ✓ Promote Safety
- ✓ Honor Values
- ✓ Give Control
- ✓ Encourage Directed Thinking
- ✓ Encourage Active Listening
- ✓ Give Positive Feedback
- ✓ Promote Reading, Writing, or Speaking

Many examples of impromptu skits can be found. For example, in the Creative Training Techniques seminar entitled Tricks for Trainers class members work in teams to present the *worst* training opening they can imagine. They are told to break all the rules. It's very effective when trainees can laugh and learn at the same time.

If more people are needed for a particular skit, have other trainees join you for the session.

TV Game Show Reviews

☑	Revisit Content
☐	Promote Safety
☑	Honor Values
☑	Give Control
☑	Encourage Directed Thinking
☑	Encourage Active Listening
☑	Give Positive Feedback
☐	Promote Reading, Writing, or Speaking

Jeopardy®, Family Feud®, Beat the Clock®, and tic-tac-toe are all great games that can be adapted easily to a wide variety of content. Think up your own questions and make some props, or obtain the software program *Game Show Pro* (see the Bibliography and Additional Resources), which enables people to play the games on a computer with all the bells and whistles. You simply enter your own content information and the computer does the scoring.

Creative Training Techniques also offers a course on the use of games in effective training. And the *Thiagi GameLetter* (Jossey-Bass/Pfeiffer) features a variety of resources.

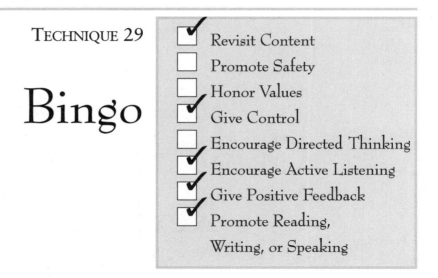

TECHNIQUE 29

Bingo

☑ Revisit Content
☐ Promote Safety
☐ Honor Values
☑ Give Control
☐ Encourage Directed Thinking
☑ Encourage Active Listening
☑ Give Positive Feedback
☑ Promote Reading,
   Writing, or Speaking

Prior to the training course, write out questions that will come up and short answers for them. No need to prepare a Bingo card in advance, although a software package is available if you want to do that (see the Bibliography and Additional Resources). Rather, at the first session, ask your learner to fill in a twenty-five square grid by randomly writing the answers only. This serves to preview the content for the learner and helps him or her become involved right away.

Throughout the training, stop at intervals and ask questions from the section just completed. Have your learner cross out the right answers on the Bingo card. When five in a row are crossed out, award a prize. At the end of the course, review the content for any answers that have not been crossed off.

Prizes and Rewards

☐	Revisit Content
☐	Promote Safety
☑	Honor Values
☐	Give Control
☑	Encourage Directed Thinking
☐	Encourage Active Listening
☑	Give Positive Feedback
☐	Promote Reading, Writing, or Speaking

During the training session, keep an ample supply of prizes and rewards to give in response to demonstrating a competency successfully (or even give a prize for coming back from a break on time if it seems appropriate).

Most companies have closets full of promotional do-dads that would be fun to award in training, or visit a novelty or toy store. Long after the training is complete, the person who was trained will have a memento of the time spent with you and what was learned.

Brainteasers

☐	Revisit Content
☐	Promote Safety
☐	Honor Values
☐	Give Control
☑	Encourage Directed Thinking
☐	Encourage Active Listening
☑	Give Positive Feedback
☐	Promote Reading, Writing, or Speaking

Brainteasers are great to use at the beginning of a session or after coming back from a break. They really get those synapses firing. However, because there is only one participant, don't put the person on the spot. Instead, share the brainteaser by describing your own experience with it and your own struggle before someone helped you find the correct answer.

Only allow the trainee to struggle with the brainteaser for a short time, and then share the answer with him or her if none is forthcoming. The *Tricks for Trainers* series and the *Wuzzles®* book from Creative Training Techniques Press are excellent sources for content-related brainteasers.

TECHNIQUE 32

Magic

☑ Revisit Content
☐ Promote Safety
☐ Honor Values
☐ Give Control
☑ Encourage Directed Thinking
☐ Encourage Active Listening
☐ Give Positive Feedback
☑ Promote Reading, Writing, or Speaking

Simple magic tricks can really break the ice and reinforce learning points too. To explore this interesting and effective training medium, look for the *Tricks for Trainers* series of books and videos (available from Creative Training Techniques Press) or purchase a few beginning books on magic and develop some tricks yourself to emphasize the learning from your one-on-one sessions.

Be sure that any tricks you use are relevant to the content and will serve as a learning aid for the trainee.

Section 3

Bonus Technique

The value of using effective openings and energizers that will engage and then re-engage training participants is undisputed. Re-energizing the learning environment also is an important consideration for the one-on-one trainer, and it is especially important in this situation to establish rapport between the trainer and the trainee. However, many popular icebreakers require more than one person or involve a level of activity that would be inappropriate and uncomfortable in a one-on-one setting.

The deck of cards that follows has been designed for you to use to bridge those sometimes-awkward opening moments, to establish rapport, or to bring the learner back to the content following lunch or a break.

For the highest level of professional materials, take the templates on the following pages to a local print shop and have them duplicate the cards onto card stock and cut and collate them for you. Enough material has been provided for eight complete decks.

Icebreaker Cards

To use the cards effectively as an icebreaker, you and the learner can take turns selecting a card at random and answering the question(s) on the card(s). Or have the trainee look through the cards and select a card for you to answer, and then you do the same. It's a great way to learn more about one another and establish rapport.

To create even more fun, add a little wholesome competition. The person answering a question can either lie or tell the truth. The other person must decide whether the answer was a lie. Award points for correct guesses. Return to the friendly competition at regular intervals throughout the training.

What is an aspect of your job that you believe most people would not believe you do?

What is an aspect of your job that you believe most people would not believe you do?

What is an aspect of your job that you believe most people would not believe you do?

What is an aspect of your job that you believe most people would not believe you do?

What is an aspect of your job that you believe most people would not believe you do?

What is an aspect of your job that you believe most people would not believe you do?

What is an aspect of your job that you believe most people would not believe you do?

What is an aspect of your job that you believe most people would not believe you do?

If you could talk to a person who had successfully performed your current job for over thirty-five years, what question(s) would you ask that person?

If you could talk to a person who had successfully performed your current job for over thirty-five years, what question(s) would you ask that person?

If you could talk to a person who had successfully performed your current job for over thirty-five years, what question(s) would you ask that person?

If you could talk to a person who had successfully performed your current job for over thirty-five years, what question(s) would you ask that person?

If you could talk to a person who had successfully performed your current job for over thirty-five years, what question(s) would you ask that person?

If you could talk to a person who had successfully performed your current job for over thirty-five years, what question(s) would you ask that person?

If you could talk to a person who had successfully performed your current job for over thirty-five years, what question(s) would you ask that person?

If you could talk to a person who had successfully performed your current job for over thirty-five years, what question(s) would you ask that person?

If you had to pick your replacement,
what qualities would you look for
in that person?

If you had to pick your replacement,
what qualities would you look for
in that person?

If you had to pick your replacement,
what qualities would you look for
in that person?

If you had to pick your replacement,
what qualities would you look for
in that person?

If you had to pick your replacement,
what qualities would you look for
in that person?

If you had to pick your replacement,
what qualities would you look for
in that person?

If you had to pick your replacement,
what qualities would you look for
in that person?

If you had to pick your replacement,
what qualities would you look for
in that person?

What is the most embarrassing
thing that's ever happened to you
during the performance of your job?

What is the most embarrassing
thing that's ever happened to you
during the performance of your job?

What is the most embarrassing
thing that's ever happened to you
during the performance of your job?

What is the most embarrassing
thing that's ever happened to you
during the performance of your job?

What is the most embarrassing
thing that's ever happened to you
during the performance of your job?

What is the most embarrassing
thing that's ever happened to you
during the performance of your job?

What is the most embarrassing
thing that's ever happened to you
during the performance of your job?

What is the most embarrassing
thing that's ever happened to you
during the performance of your job?

What's a job-related
reoccurring nightmare you have?

What's a job-related
reoccurring nightmare you have?

What's a job-related
reoccurring nightmare you have?

What's a job-related
reoccurring nightmare you have?

What's a job-related
reoccurring nightmare you have?

What's a job-related
reoccurring nightmare you have?

What's a job-related
reoccurring nightmare you have?

What's a job-related
reoccurring nightmare you have?

All humility aside, what would you say has been your greatest accomplishment in your current job?

All humility aside, what would you say has been your greatest accomplishment in your current job?

All humility aside, what would you say has been your greatest accomplishment in your current job?

All humility aside, what would you say has been your greatest accomplishment in your current job?

All humility aside, what would you say has been your greatest accomplishment in your current job?

All humility aside, what would you say has been your greatest accomplishment in your current job?

All humility aside, what would you say has been your greatest accomplishment in your current job?

All humility aside, what would you say has been your greatest accomplishment in your current job?

What book have you read that
really helped you in your
job performance?

What book have you read that
really helped you in your
job performance?

What book have you read that
really helped you in your
job performance?

What book have you read that
really helped you in your
job performance?

What book have you read that
really helped you in your
job performance?

What book have you read that
really helped you in your
job performance?

What book have you read that
really helped you in your
job performance?

What book have you read that
really helped you in your
job performance?

If you started a support group for others who perform your job, what would be one issue that someone would surely bring up?

If you started a support group for others who perform your job, what would be one issue that someone would surely bring up?

If you started a support group for others who perform your job, what would be one issue that someone would surely bring up?

If you started a support group for others who perform your job, what would be one issue that someone would surely bring up?

If you started a support group for others who perform your job, what would be one issue that someone would surely bring up?

If you started a support group for others who perform your job, what would be one issue that someone would surely bring up?

If you started a support group for others who perform your job, what would be one issue that someone would surely bring up?

If you started a support group for others who perform your job, what would be one issue that someone would surely bring up?

How does your job differ from what you thought it would be like before you assumed the position?

How does your job differ from what you thought it would be like before you assumed the position?

How does your job differ from what you thought it would be like before you assumed the position?

How does your job differ from what you thought it would be like before you assumed the position?

How does your job differ from what you thought it would be like before you assumed the position?

How does your job differ from what you thought it would be like before you assumed the position?

How does your job differ from what you thought it would be like before you assumed the position?

How does your job differ from what you thought it would be like before you assumed the position?

If you could have a personal
twenty-four-hour consulting
hotline to anyone in the industry,
who would it be?

If you could have a personal
twenty-four-hour consulting
hotline to anyone in the industry,
who would it be?

If you could have a personal
twenty-four-hour consulting
hotline to anyone in the industry,
who would it be?

If you could have a personal
twenty-four-hour consulting
hotline to anyone in the industry,
who would it be?

If you could have a personal
twenty-four-hour consulting
hotline to anyone in the industry,
who would it be?

If you could have a personal
twenty-four-hour consulting
hotline to anyone in the industry,
who would it be?

If you could have a personal
twenty-four-hour consulting
hotline to anyone in the industry,
who would it be?

If you could have a personal
twenty-four-hour consulting
hotline to anyone in the industry,
who would it be?

If you started a magazine for people who perform your job, what would you call it? Why?

If you started a magazine for people who perform your job, what would you call it? Why?

If you started a magazine for people who perform your job, what would you call it? Why?

If you started a magazine for people who perform your job, what would you call it? Why?

If you started a magazine for people who perform your job, what would you call it? Why?

If you started a magazine for people who perform your job, what would you call it? Why?

If you started a magazine for people who perform your job, what would you call it? Why?

If you started a magazine for people who perform your job, what would you call it? Why?

If you could wave a wand and have your job performed perfectly, what would the result look like?

If you could wave a wand and have your job performed perfectly, what would the result look like?

If you could wave a wand and have your job performed perfectly, what would the result look like?

If you could wave a wand and have your job performed perfectly, what would the result look like?

If you could wave a wand and have your job performed perfectly, what would the result look like?

If you could wave a wand and have your job performed perfectly, what would the result look like?

If you could wave a wand and have your job performed perfectly, what would the result look like?

If you could wave a wand and have your job performed perfectly, what would the result look like?

If everyone who performed your
job formed a softball team,
what would the mascot be? Why?

If everyone who performed your
job formed a softball team,
what would the mascot be? Why?

If everyone who performed your
job formed a softball team,
what would the mascot be? Why?

If everyone who performed your
job formed a softball team,
what would the mascot be? Why?

If everyone who performed your
job formed a softball team,
what would the mascot be? Why?

If everyone who performed your
job formed a softball team,
what would the mascot be? Why?

If everyone who performed your
job formed a softball team,
what would the mascot be? Why?

If everyone who performed your
job formed a softball team,
what would the mascot be? Why?

What hour during the workday seems
to go the fastest? Why?

What hour during the workday seems
to go the fastest? Why?

What hour during the workday seems
to go the fastest? Why?

What hour during the workday seems
to go the fastest? Why?

What hour during the workday seems
to go the fastest? Why?

What hour during the workday seems
to go the fastest? Why?

What hour during the workday seems
to go the fastest? Why?

What hour during the workday seems
to go the fastest? Why?

What is the most common
question people ask when
they hear what you do?

What is the most common
question people ask when
they hear what you do?

What is the most common
question people ask when
they hear what you do?

What is the most common
question people ask when
they hear what you do?

What is the most common
question people ask when
they hear what you do?

What is the most common
question people ask when
they hear what you do?

What is the most common
question people ask when
they hear what you do?

What is the most common
question people ask when
they hear what you do?

What color best describes your job?
Why?

What color best describes your job?
Why?

What color best describes your job?
Why?

What color best describes your job?
Why?

What color best describes your job?
Why?

What color best describes your job?
Why?

What color best describes your job?
Why?

What color best describes your job?
Why?

What hour during the workday
seems to go the slowest? Why?

What hour during the workday
seems to go the slowest? Why?

What hour during the workday
seems to go the slowest? Why?

What hour during the workday
seems to go the slowest? Why?

What hour during the workday
seems to go the slowest? Why?

What hour during the workday
seems to go the slowest? Why?

What hour during the workday
seems to go the slowest? Why?

What hour during the workday
seems to go the slowest? Why?

If you could move with the speed
of light, for what one aspect of your
job would you use this ability?

If you could move with the speed
of light, for what one aspect of your
job would you use this ability?

If you could move with the speed
of light, for what one aspect of your
job would you use this ability?

If you could move with the speed
of light, for what one aspect of your
job would you use this ability?

If you could move with the speed
of light, for what one aspect of your
job would you use this ability?

If you could move with the speed
of light, for what one aspect of your
job would you use this ability?

If you could move with the speed
of light, for what one aspect of your
job would you use this ability?

If you could move with the speed
of light, for what one aspect of your
job would you use this ability?

How could the power to become
invisible help you in your job?

How could the power to become
invisible help you in your job?

How could the power to become
invisible help you in your job?

How could the power to become
invisible help you in your job?

How could the power to become
invisible help you in your job?

How could the power to become
invisible help you in your job?

How could the power to become
invisible help you in your job?

How could the power to become
invisible help you in your job?

If you could wish for yourself
one superpower in order to
perform your job more successfully,
what would it be?

If you could wish for yourself
one superpower in order to
perform your job more successfully,
what would it be?

If you could wish for yourself
one superpower in order to
perform your job more successfully,
what would it be?

If you could wish for yourself
one superpower in order to
perform your job more successfully,
what would it be?

If you could wish for yourself
one superpower in order to
perform your job more successfully,
what would it be?

If you could wish for yourself
one superpower in order to
perform your job more successfully,
what would it be?

If you could wish for yourself
one superpower in order to
perform your job more successfully,
what would it be?

If you could wish for yourself
one superpower in order to
perform your job more successfully,
what would it be?

If you carried a packet of tranquilizers with you, during what part of your job would you be most likely to use one?

If you carried a packet of tranquilizers with you, during what part of your job would you be most likely to use one?

If you carried a packet of tranquilizers with you, during what part of your job would you be most likely to use one?

If you carried a packet of tranquilizers with you, during what part of your job would you be most likely to use one?

If you carried a packet of tranquilizers with you, during what part of your job would you be most likely to use one?

If you carried a packet of tranquilizers with you, during what part of your job would you be most likely to use one?

If you carried a packet of tranquilizers with you, during what part of your job would you be most likely to use one?

If you carried a packet of tranquilizers with you, during what part of your job would you be most likely to use one?

What is one aspect of your job that feels as though it's never done?

What is one aspect of your job that feels as though it's never done?

What is one aspect of your job that feels as though it's never done?

What is one aspect of your job that feels as though it's never done?

What is one aspect of your job that feels as though it's never done?

What is one aspect of your job that feels as though it's never done?

What is one aspect of your job that feels as though it's never done?

What is one aspect of your job that feels as though it's never done?

What is it about your job that makes it so that not just anyone can do it?

What is it about your job that makes it so that not just anyone can do it?

What is it about your job that makes it so that not just anyone can do it?

What is it about your job that makes it so that not just anyone can do it?

What is it about your job that makes it so that not just anyone can do it?

What is it about your job that makes it so that not just anyone can do it?

What is it about your job that makes it so that not just anyone can do it?

What title would you give yourself
to communicate your responsibilities
more accurately to others?

What title would you give yourself
to communicate your responsibilities
more accurately to others?

What title would you give yourself
to communicate your responsibilities
more accurately to others?

What title would you give yourself
to communicate your responsibilities
more accurately to others?

What title would you give yourself
to communicate your responsibilities
more accurately to others?

What title would you give yourself
to communicate your responsibilities
more accurately to others?

What title would you give yourself
to communicate your responsibilities
more accurately to others?

What title would you give yourself
to communicate your responsibilities
more accurately to others?

What circumstances moved you
into your present job?

What circumstances moved you
into your present job?

What circumstances moved you
into your present job?

What circumstances moved you
into your present job?

What circumstances moved you
into your present job?

What circumstances moved you
into your present job?

What circumstances moved you
into your present job?

What circumstances moved you
into your present job?

Of all the characters from childhood fairy tales (Snow White, the Three Bears, the Three Little Pigs, the Seven Dwarfs, etc.), which would be most successful at your job?

Of all the characters from childhood fairy tales (Snow White, the Three Bears, the Three Little Pigs, the Seven Dwarfs, etc.), which would be most successful at your job?

Of all the characters from childhood fairy tales (Snow White, the Three Bears, the Three Little Pigs, the Seven Dwarfs, etc.), which would be most successful at your job?

Of all the characters from childhood fairy tales (Snow White, the Three Bears, the Three Little Pigs, the Seven Dwarfs, etc.), which would be most successful at your job?

Of all the characters from childhood fairy tales (Snow White, the Three Bears, the Three Little Pigs, the Seven Dwarfs, etc.), which would be most successful at your job?

Of all the characters from childhood fairy tales (Snow White, the Three Bears, the Three Little Pigs, the Seven Dwarfs, etc.), which would be most successful at your job?

Of all the characters from childhood fairy tales (Snow White, the Three Bears, the Three Little Pigs, the Seven Dwarfs, etc.), which would be most successful at your job?

Of all the characters from childhood fairy tales (Snow White, the Three Bears, the Three Little Pigs, the Seven Dwarfs, etc.), which would be most successful at your job?

Of all the cartoon characters
you've ever seen, which one would
probably be most successful in your
job position? Why?

Of all the cartoon characters
you've ever seen, which one would
probably be most successful in your
job position? Why?

Of all the cartoon characters
you've ever seen, which one would
probably be most successful in your
job position? Why?

Of all the cartoon characters
you've ever seen, which one would
probably be most successful in your
job position? Why?

Of all the cartoon characters
you've ever seen, which one would
probably be most successful in your
job position? Why?

Of all the cartoon characters
you've ever seen, which one would
probably be most successful in your
job position? Why?

Of all the cartoon characters
you've ever seen, which one would
probably be most successful in your
job position? Why?

Of all the cartoon characters
you've ever seen, which one would
probably be most successful in your
job position? Why?

How long do you think someone could reasonably keep doing your present job and still enjoy it?

How long do you think someone could reasonably keep doing your present job and still enjoy it?

How long do you think someone could reasonably keep doing your present job and still enjoy it?

How long do you think someone could reasonably keep doing your present job and still enjoy it?

How long do you think someone could reasonably keep doing your present job and still enjoy it?

How long do you think someone could reasonably keep doing your present job and still enjoy it?

How long do you think someone could reasonably keep doing your present job and still enjoy it?

How long do you think someone could reasonably keep doing your present job and still enjoy it?

Which one of your relatives (living or deceased) would probably have been most successful at your job? Why?

Which one of your relatives (living or deceased) would probably have been most successful at your job? Why?

Which one of your relatives (living or deceased) would probably have been most successful at your job? Why?

Which one of your relatives (living or deceased) would probably have been most successful at your job? Why?

Which one of your relatives (living or deceased) would probably have been most successful at your job? Why?

Which one of your relatives (living or deceased) would probably have been most successful at your job? Why?

Which one of your relatives (living or deceased) would probably have been most successful at your job? Why?

Which one of your relatives (living or deceased) would probably have been most successful at your job? Why?

How long does one need to
do your job before being
consistently successful?

How long does one need to
do your job before being
consistently successful?

How long does one need to
do your job before being
consistently successful?

How long does one need to
do your job before being
consistently successful?

How long does one need to
do your job before being
consistently successful?

How long does one need to
do your job before being
consistently successful?

How long does one need to
do your job before being
consistently successful?

How long does one need to
do your job before being
consistently successful?

Of all the famous historical people you know about, which one would probably have been most successful at your present job? Why?

Of all the famous historical people you know about, which one would probably have been most successful at your present job? Why?

Of all the famous historical people you know about, which one would probably have been most successful at your present job? Why?

Of all the famous historical people you know about, which one would probably have been most successful at your present job? Why?

Of all the famous historical people you know about, which one would probably have been most successful at your present job? Why?

Of all the famous historical people you know about, which one would probably have been most successful at your present job? Why?

Of all the famous historical people you know about, which one would probably have been most successful at your present job? Why?

Of all the famous historical people you know about, which one would probably have been most successful at your present job? Why?

If you wrote a commercial to sell other people on applying for your job, what three benefits would you highlight for the prospective applicants?

If you wrote a commercial to sell other people on applying for your job, what three benefits would you highlight for the prospective applicants?

If you wrote a commercial to sell other people on applying for your job, what three benefits would you highlight for the prospective applicants?

If you wrote a commercial to sell other people on applying for your job, what three benefits would you highlight for the prospective applicants?

If you wrote a commercial to sell other people on applying for your job, what three benefits would you highlight for the prospective applicants?

If you wrote a commercial to sell other people on applying for your job, what three benefits would you highlight for the prospective applicants?

If you wrote a commercial to sell other people on applying for your job, what three benefits would you highlight for the prospective applicants?

If you wrote a commercial to sell other people on applying for your job, what three benefits would you highlight for the prospective applicants?

What qualities of a child would
be helpful in successfully
accomplishing your job?

What qualities of a child would
be helpful in successfully
accomplishing your job?

What qualities of a child would
be helpful in successfully
accomplishing your job?

What qualities of a child would
be helpful in successfully
accomplishing your job?

What qualities of a child would
be helpful in successfully
accomplishing your job?

What qualities of a child would
be helpful in successfully
accomplishing your job?

What qualities of a child would
be helpful in successfully
accomplishing your job?

What qualities of a child would
be helpful in successfully
accomplishing your job?

If money were no object, what would you purchase to help you be more successful in your job?

If money were no object, what would you purchase to help you be more successful in your job?

If money were no object, what would you purchase to help you be more successful in your job?

If money were no object, what would you purchase to help you be more successful in your job?

If money were no object, what would you purchase to help you be more successful in your job?

If money were no object, what would you purchase to help you be more successful in your job?

If money were no object, what would you purchase to help you be more successful in your job?

If money were no object, what would you purchase to help you be more successful in your job?

What piece of fruit does your job
most resemble? Why?

What piece of fruit does your job
most resemble? Why?

What piece of fruit does your job
most resemble? Why?

What piece of fruit does your job
most resemble? Why?

What piece of fruit does your job
most resemble? Why?

What piece of fruit does your job
most resemble? Why?

What piece of fruit does your job
most resemble? Why?

What piece of fruit does your job
most resemble? Why?

What aspect of your job do you find
most challenging?

What aspect of your job do you find
most challenging?

What aspect of your job do you find
most challenging?

What aspect of your job do you find
most challenging?

What aspect of your job do you find
most challenging?

What aspect of your job do you find
most challenging?

What aspect of your job do you find
most challenging?

What aspect of your job do you find
most challenging?

If you were designing a college curriculum to prepare people for your job, what would be three of the course titles?

If you were designing a college curriculum to prepare people for your job, what would be three of the course titles?

If you were designing a college curriculum to prepare people for your job, what would be three of the course titles?

If you were designing a college curriculum to prepare people for your job, what would be three of the course titles?

If you were designing a college curriculum to prepare people for your job, what would be three of the course titles?

If you were designing a college curriculum to prepare people for your job, what would be three of the course titles?

If you were designing a college curriculum to prepare people for your job, what would be three of the course titles?

If you were designing a college curriculum to prepare people for your job, what would be three of the course titles?

If you were training a novice to do your job, what is one piece of advice you'd be sure to give?

If you were training a novice to do your job, what is one piece of advice you'd be sure to give?

If you were training a novice to do your job, what is one piece of advice you'd be sure to give?

If you were training a novice to do your job, what is one piece of advice you'd be sure to give?

If you were training a novice to do your job, what is one piece of advice you'd be sure to give?

If you were training a novice to do your job, what is one piece of advice you'd be sure to give?

If you were training a novice to do your job, what is one piece of advice you'd be sure to give?

If you were training a novice to do your job, what is one piece of advice you'd be sure to give?

What about your childhood helped prepare you for the responsibilities you currently have on the job?

What about your childhood helped prepare you for the responsibilities you currently have on the job?

What about your childhood helped prepare you for the responsibilities you currently have on the job?

What about your childhood helped prepare you for the responsibilities you currently have on the job?

What about your childhood helped prepare you for the responsibilities you currently have on the job?

What about your childhood helped prepare you for the responsibilities you currently have on the job?

What about your childhood helped prepare you for the responsibilities you currently have on the job?

What about your childhood helped prepare you for the responsibilities you currently have on the job?

If you had to describe your job using just one word, what would that word be?

If you had to describe your job using just one word, what would that word be?

If you had to describe your job using just one word, what would that word be?

If you had to describe your job using just one word, what would that word be?

If you had to describe your job using just one word, what would that word be?

If you had to describe your job using just one word, what would that word be?

If you had to describe your job using just one word, what would that word be?

If you had to describe your job using just one word, what would that word be?

How many years, months, weeks,
or days have you been in your
present position?

How many years, months, weeks,
or days have you been in your
present position?

How many years, months, weeks,
or days have you been in your
present position?

How many years, months, weeks,
or days have you been in your
present position?

How many years, months, weeks,
or days have you been in your
present position?

How many years, months, weeks,
or days have you been in your
present position?

How many years, months, weeks,
or days have you been in your
present position?

How many years, months, weeks,
or days have you been in your
present position?

If you wrote a book about your job experiences, what would the title be? Why?

If you wrote a book about your job experiences, what would the title be? Why?

If you wrote a book about your job experiences, what would the title be? Why?

If you wrote a book about your job experiences, what would the title be? Why?

If you wrote a book about your job experiences, what would the title be? Why?

If you wrote a book about your job experiences, what would the title be? Why?

If you wrote a book about your job experiences, what would the title be? Why?

If you wrote a book about your job experiences, what would the title be? Why?

At your retirement party,
what do you hope is said
about your job performance?

At your retirement party,
what do you hope is said
about your job performance?

At your retirement party,
what do you hope is said
about your job performance?

At your retirement party,
what do you hope is said
about your job performance?

At your retirement party,
what do you hope is said
about your job performance?

At your retirement party,
what do you hope is said
about your job performance?

At your retirement party,
what do you hope is said
about your job performance?

At your retirement party,
what do you hope is said
about your job performance?

If suddenly you were required to do one aspect of your job over and over again, which aspect would you wish that to be?

If suddenly you were required to do one aspect of your job over and over again, which aspect would you wish that to be?

If suddenly you were required to do one aspect of your job over and over again, which aspect would you wish that to be?

If suddenly you were required to do one aspect of your job over and over again, which aspect would you wish that to be?

If suddenly you were required to do one aspect of your job over and over again, which aspect would you wish that to be?

If suddenly you were required to do one aspect of your job over and over again, which aspect would you wish that to be?

If suddenly you were required to do one aspect of your job over and over again, which aspect would you wish that to be?

If suddenly you were required to do one aspect of your job over and over again, which aspect would you wish that to be?

How could being in more than one place at a time help you on the job?

How could being in more than one place at a time help you on the job?

How could being in more than one place at a time help you on the job?

How could being in more than one place at a time help you on the job?

How could being in more than one place at a time help you on the job?

How could being in more than one place at a time help you on the job?

How could being in more than one place at a time help you on the job?

How could being in more than one place at a time help you on the job?

If you designed your own
evaluation sheet for your present
job, what three categories should
be included for sure?

If you designed your own
evaluation sheet for your present
job, what three categories should
be included for sure?

If you designed your own
evaluation sheet for your present
job, what three categories should
be included for sure?

If you designed your own
evaluation sheet for your present
job, what three categories should
be included for sure?

If you designed your own
evaluation sheet for your present
job, what three categories should
be included for sure?

If you designed your own
evaluation sheet for your present
job, what three categories should
be included for sure?

If you designed your own
evaluation sheet for your present
job, what three categories should
be included for sure?

If you designed your own
evaluation sheet for your present
job, what three categories should
be included for sure?

What is the longest amount of
time you know anyone has remained
in a job such as yours?

What is the longest amount of
time you know anyone has remained
in a job such as yours?

What is the longest amount of
time you know anyone has remained
in a job such as yours?

What is the longest amount of
time you know anyone has remained
in a job such as yours?

What is the longest amount of
time you know anyone has remained
in a job such as yours?

What is the longest amount of
time you know anyone has remained
in a job such as yours?

What is the longest amount of
time you know anyone has remained
in a job such as yours?

What is the longest amount of
time you know anyone has remained
in a job such as yours?

How could having x-ray vision help you in your job performance?

How could having x-ray vision help you in your job performance?

How could having x-ray vision help you in your job performance?

How could having x-ray vision help you in your job performance?

How could having x-ray vision help you in your job performance?

How could having x-ray vision help you in your job performance?

How could having x-ray vision help you in your job performance?

How could having x-ray vision help you in your job performance?

How would the ability to make time go backward help you in your job?

How would the ability to make time go backward help you in your job?

How would the ability to make time go backward help you in your job?

How would the ability to make time go backward help you in your job?

How would the ability to make time go backward help you in your job?

How would the ability to make time go backward help you in your job?

How would the ability to make time go backward help you in your job?

How would the ability to make time go backward help you in your job?

If you could change one component
of your job description, what
would it be?

If you could change one component
of your job description, what
would it be?

If you could change one component
of your job description, what
would it be?

If you could change one component
of your job description, what
would it be?

If you could change one component
of your job description, what
would it be?

If you could change one component
of your job description, what
would it be?

If you could change one component
of your job description, what
would it be?

If you could change one component
of your job description, what
would it be?

If you started a magazine for people who perform your job, what would be the title of one article in the first issue?

If you started a magazine for people who perform your job, what would be the title of one article in the first issue?

If you started a magazine for people who perform your job, what would be the title of one article in the first issue?

If you started a magazine for people who perform your job, what would be the title of one article in the first issue?

If you started a magazine for people who perform your job, what would be the title of one article in the first issue?

If you started a magazine for people who perform your job, what would be the title of one article in the first issue?

If you started a magazine for people who perform your job, what would be the title of one article in the first issue?

If you started a magazine for people who perform your job, what would be the title of one article in the first issue?

Bibliography and Additional Resources

Books, Music, Software, and Videos

Creative Training Techniques Handbook by Bob Pike. Minneapolis, MN: Lakewood Publications, 1994.

>*The* textbook for training excellence! With over two hundred pages of information regarding the participant-centered approach to training, this book is a must have for every trainer's library. Chapter titles include Visual Aids, Creating Effective Resource Materials, Presentation Techniques, and Learner Motivation.

Crosswords & More Software™, Expert Software.

>Designs crossword puzzles with ease. Also has a "Find the Word" design component for making "circle the word in the letter grid" puzzles customized to your content!

Dealing with Difficult Participants by Bob Pike and Dave Arch. San Francisco, CA, and Minneapolis, MN: Jossey-Bass/Pfeiffer and Creative Training Techniques Press, 1997.

>If you deal with difficult participants in your training sessions, this is the book for you. The book contains 127 proven methods for dealing with 15 types of difficult participants.

Evaluating Training Programs by Donald Kirkpatrick. San Francisco, CA: Berrett-Koehler, 1994.

> Providing a clear explanation of the four levels of training assessment, this book has become *the* textbook for effective measurement of training effectiveness.

Evaluation by Sandra Merwin. San Francisco, CA, and Minneapolis, MN: Jossey-Bass/Pfeiffer and Creative Training Techniques Press, 1994.

> This excellent book examines the effective design of pre-test and post-test questions, as well as how to choose the most effective method(s) of evaluating your training. Written in simple, clear language, the book includes many ready-to-use examples.

Gameshow Pro Software. Learning Ware Inc.

> This software package enables you to pre-program questions into Jeopardy®, Tic-Tac-Toe, or Family Feud® formats, complete with all the bells and whistles and automatic scoring. Great for team competition review.

Powerful Presentation Music (Volumes 1 & 2). Minneapolis, MN: Creative Training Techniques Press, 1994.

> Each of these volumes contains powerful music for use in the training room. Great for setting the right mood and putting energy into the session, each selection is royalty-free, avoiding potentially costly copyright issues. Each volume contains three cassettes for a total of ninety minutes of music per volume.

Red Hot Handouts! by Dave Arch. San Francisco, CA, and Minneapolis, MN: Jossey-Bass/Pfeiffer and Creative Training Techniques Press, 1997.

> The focus of this book is the creative design and use of handouts in presentations. You will find many ideas for more effective handouts that your participants will keep and even show others! These handout ideas customize to any content!

Showmanship for Presenters by Dave Arch. San Francisco, CA, and Minneapolis, MN: Jossey-Bass/Pfeiffer and Creative Training Techniques Press, 1997.

> This volume examines forty-nine techniques used by famous entertainers that have direct application to the training room. You'll discover powerful ways to use the front of your room based on staging principles, the under-utilized power of unveiling, and forty-seven others.

The *Thiagi GameLetter,* edited by Sivasailam Thiagarajan. San Francisco, CA: Jossey-Bass/Pfeiffer.

> Designed to help trainers, managers, and others use interactive techniques to improve human performance. Provides a wide variety of training games, simulations, and other creative methods to deliver results quickly and effectively.

Top Ten of Everything by Russell Ash. New York: Dorling Kindersley, 1999.

> Published with new statistics each year, this book of lists is excellent for designing trivia questions.

Tricks for Trainers (Volumes 1 & 2) by Dave Arch. San Francisco, CA, and Minneapolis, MN: Jossey-Bass/Pfeiffer and Creative Training Techniques Press, 1994, 1996.

> These books explain how to do simple training magic tricks with everyday objects at your fingertips; they also include reproducible transparency brain-teaser masters. These books have become a classic for the trainer's library.

Tricks for Trainers Video Library by Dave Arch. Des Moines, IA: Smart Choice Videos, 1996.

> This three-volume video set teaches completely different training magic from the books and, due to its visual nature, makes the learning fun and easy! Each tape is approximately thirty minutes in length, for a total of sixty different magic tricks.

Wuzzles for Presenters. San Francisco, CA, and Minneapolis, MN: Jossey-Bass/Pfeiffer and Creative Training Techniques Press, 1997.

> A mind-boggling collection of 464 different word puzzles organized in categories by content applications, such as customer service, technical training, and educational.

Zingo Bingo Software. Bloomington, IN: Workshops by Thiagi.

> This software creates Bingo cards for use during training activities. When you enter twenty-five different answers to your own personal content questions, the software immediately reorganizes those twenty-five components into a possible 64,000 different combinations. You can then print as many different Bingo cards as you need, depending on the size of your audience.

Seminars

Creative Training Techniques™ Seminar

> Publicly presented over one hundred times each year throughout the United States, this two-day seminar will show you how to transform your training into a more participant-centered learning experience. For a comprehensive seminar brochure call (800) 383-9210.

Creative Training Techniques for One-on-One Trainers

> This one-day in-house offering uses this book as its main text and guides participants through the design and delivery of effective one-on-one training, including the creating of specific training tools and activities for use in that training. Call the number above.

Games and Graphics Seminar

Offered at the Creative Training Techniques Annual Conference and as a customized training program, this one-day or two-day program helps participants brainstorm ways to develop and utilize graphics effectively, as well as how to adapt common game-show formats to their content. For more information call (800) 383-9210.

Tricks for Trainers Seminar by Dave Arch

This one-day or two-day seminar is offered at the Creative Training Techniques Annual Conference and as a customized training program. Get hands-on experience with the activities presented in the above books and videos. Call (800) 383-9210 for more information.

Web Sites

Creative Training Techniques World Wide Web Site

A resource center at *http://www.creativetrainingtech.com* that is ever-changing. On the site, you will find a section entitled Puzzlers for Presenters, from which you can download monthly brain-teaser puzzle transparency masters that are perfect as a warm-up activity.

Thiagi Web Site

A collection of training games, puzzles, etc. *http://www.thiagi.com.*

About the Authors

Bob Pike, CSP, CPAE

Bob Pike has developed and implemented training programs for business, industry, government, and the professions since 1969. He began his career as a representative for Master Education Industries, where he moved up to become a senior vice president. His responsibilities included developing an intensive three-week Master Training Academy, which covered all phases of sales training, management development, communications, motivation/platform skills, and business operations. During his five years as vice president of Personal Dynamics, Inc., that company grew from fewer than four thousand enrollments per year to more than eighty thousand. He pioneered undergraduate and graduate credit for training on a national basis. As CEO and founder of Creative Training Techniques Press and Creative Training Techniques International, Inc., Bob leads sessions over 150 days per year, covering the topics of leadership, attitudes, motivation, communication, decision making, problem solving, personal and organizational effectiveness, conflict management, team building, and managerial productivity. More than 75,000 trainers have attended the Creative Training Techniques' seminar. As a consultant Bob has worked with such organizations as Pfizer, Upjohn, Caesar Boardwalk Regency, *Exhibitor Magazine,* Hallmark Cards, and IBM.

A member of the American Society for Training and Development (ASTD) since 1972, Bob has been active in many capacities. He is currently serving on the Board of Directors for the National Speakers'

Association (NSA) and the International Alliance of Learning. He has presented at regional and national ASTD and Training conferences. In 1991 he was granted the professional designation of Certified Speaking Professional (CSP) by the National Speakers Association (NSA). In 1999 he was inducted into the NSA CPAE (Council of Peers Award of Excellence) Speaker's Hall of Fame. Since 1980, he has been listed in *Who's Who in the Midwest* and is listed in the current edition of *Who's Who in Finance and Industry.* Over the years, Bob has contributed to many magazines such as *Training, The Personnel Administrator,* and *The Self-Development Journal.* He is editor of the *Creative Training Techniques Newsletter* and is author of *The Creative Training Techniques Handbook, Developing, Marketing, and Promoting Successful Seminars and Workshops,* and *Improving Managerial Productivity.*

Lynn Solem

Since December of 1986, Lynn has delivered over 6,000 hours of Creative Training Techniques®. She has delivered specialty aspects of Creative Training Techniques for Lakewood Publications' Best of America and Total Trainer conferences. Lynn has created and delivered seminars and workshops on such topics as sales skills, interpersonal communications, team building, leadership skills, communication styles, problem solving, and managing service as a corporate asset. She began her career in radio.

Formerly the executive vice president and chief executive officer at Personal Dynamics, Inc., she was responsible for developing and marketing materials used in seminars, training, and workshop settings. Lynn has received many national awards, been selected as "Outstanding Young Woman of America," and been inducted into the United Nations Hall of Fame.

Lynn's consulting clients have included General Dynamics, EDS, MCI Pacific and Midwest Divisions, the U.S. Postal Service, IBM, Pennsylvania Power and Light, the U.S. Bureau of Patents, the Houston Independent School District, the National School Board Association, the Federal Bureau of Prisons, Southwestern Bell Telephone, and Consolidated Edison.

Dave Arch

Dave Arch, best-selling author and nationally acclaimed training conference speaker, is the author of seven videos and resource books for the training industry, including *Tricks for Trainers* (Volumes 1 and 2), in addition to his popular monthly column in the *Creative Training Techniques Newsletter*.

Drawing on twenty-five years of training experience, Dave travels for CTT, customizing and presenting four different participant-centered train-the-trainer seminars and keynotes, including the cutting-edge seminar entitled Creative Training Techniques for Distance Learning.

Dave's clients include The Nabisco Company, US West Communications, the U.S. Postal Service, The Internal Revenue Service, Kimberly-Clark, The National Education Association, Canada Postal Service, Napa Auto Parts, and The United States Central Intelligence Agency.

More great resources from Jossey-Bass/Pfeiffer!

End your sessions with a BANG!

Lynn Solem & Bob Pike

50 Creative Training Closers

They'll forget you as soon as you walk out the door—unless you make your training memorable. This essential resource is your way to make your mark. Fifty ways to close your training sessions and presentations so they won't forget you—or your training.

Many trainers start training sessions memorably with a rousing icebreaker, or with a spirited overview of what's to follow. But you're probably letting the ends slip through your fingers. Some trainers conclude training sessions by looking at their watches and saying, "Oh, time's up! Goodbye!" By trailing off with a whisper, you're missing an opportunity to reinforce your training. You're helping your participants to forget everything you've taught them. Stop this brain drain by ending with a bang! This invaluable book is packed with practical closers.

You get activities great for:

- *Reviewing* material
- *Celebrating* success
- *Motivating* participants . . . and more!

Solem and Pike show you all the essentials, and preparation is quick and easy. So little time to invest for such a HUGE payoff! This book is training dynamite—make it your secret weapon today.

paperback / 96 pages

50 Creative Training Closers
Item #F439

Bob Pike & Dave Arch

Dealing with Difficult Participants

127 Practical Strategies for Minimizing Resistance and Maximizing Results in Your Presentations

Everyone knows them . . . but almost no one knows how to deal with them. Difficult participants. The "latecomer." The "know-it-all." The "confused." What do you do? Train-the-trainer master Bob Pike and magician/trainer Dave Arch have the answers.

Learn to deal with types such as:

- The Preoccupied
- The Socializer
- The Introvert
- The Bored
- The Domineering
- The Unqualified
- The Skeptic
- The Sleeper . . . and others!

Don't let difficult participants get the best of you. You can't afford not to pick up this engaging book. Maximize the learning potential in all your presentations with *Dealing With Difficult Participants*!

paperback / 150 pages

Dealing with Difficult Participants
Item #F244

To order, please contact your local bookstore, call us toll-free at 1-800-274-4434, or visit us on the Web at www.pfeiffer.com.

WIN *Rave Reviews*
on your next **Presentation**

"I have never felt so enthusiastic about a program! This workshop is a MUST for any trainer, regardless of level of experience."

Susan Russell, Bank One

Do you talk so people really listen?

Bob Pike's Creative Training Techniques™ Seminar

Find out why over 65,000 trainers love Creative Training Techniques. What makes this seminar so different? You'll learn how to get your participants enthusiastically involved in the training. By creating an interactive learning environment, you'll watch the attendees excitement go up and up and up. The result? Your group will easily learn twice as much. When they apply their new skills on the job, you'll see dramatic results.

Learn a revolutionary training approach—Participant-Centered Training. This teaching style is far more effective than traditional lecture-based training. Over 65,000 trainers world-wide have attended this seminar and applied these participant-centered training techniques to their work environments. More effective training means a more valuable and effective work force. Register today so you can get rave reviews on your next presentation. Over 140 public seminars are scheduled in 40 different cities each year.

In-house Training Seminars

Customized programs for trainers, sales staff, and technical presenters developed for 100s of organizations. Give us a call so we can discuss how to help your company increase work force performance by maximizing the impact of your training. Just a few of our clients who have brought Creative Training Techniques programs in-house:

American Express • AT&T • GE Plastics • State Farm Insurance • 3M • Tonka Corporation

Creative Solutions Catalog
Insider's Tips to Double the Impact of Your Presentation

Filled with fun, stimulating, creative resources including games, magic, music, wuzzles, books, tapes, videos, software, presentation graphics—everything you need to make your presentation an absolute winner.

1-800-383-9210
www.cttbobpike.com

Creative Training Techniques International, Inc. • 7620 W. 78th Street, Mpls. MN 55439 • (612) 829-1954 • Fax (612) 829-0260

Bob Pike's
Creative Training Techniques™
Train-the-Trainer Conference

*The only conference dedicated exclusively
to the participant-centered approach to training*

- Learn about the revolutionary, participant-centered training approach—the breakthrough alternative to lecture-based training
- See the nation's leading training consultants model their very best participant-centered activities
- Experience the power of participant-centered techniques to dramatically increase retention
- Learn about innovative training transfer techniques adopted by leading Fortune 500 companies
- Discover powerful management strategies that clearly demonstrate the business results for your training programs

Just a few of the companies who have sent groups (not just individuals) to the Conference

American Express • AT&T • Caterpillar • First Bank
Southern Nuclear Operating Company • State Farm • United HealthCare • US West

Rave Reviews!

"I refer to my conference workbook all the time. I've shared the techniques with my trainers, and my own evaluations have improved. Our needs analysis now produces actionable input. My comfort level with our line managers has increased—at my first meeting with them where I used what I learned at the conference, they applauded. Now that's positive feedback!"
> Gretchen Gospodarek, Training Manager, **TCF Bank Wisconsin**

"For any trainer who wants to move beyond lecture-based training, I recommend Bob Pike's participant-centered seminars and in-house consultants."
> Ken Blanchard, Co-Author of *The One-Minute Manager*

"Bob Pike is creating a new standard in the industry by which all other programs will soon be measured."
> Elliott Masie, President, **The MASIE Center**

Visit our Web site: www.cttbobpike.com to learn more about the Conference, Creative Training Techniques International, Inc. or the Participant-Centered Training approach.

1–800–383–9210
www.cttbobpike.com

Creative Training Techniques International, Inc. • 7620 W. 78th St., Mpls., MN 55439 • 612-829-1954 • Fax 612-829-0260

13 Questions to Ask *Before* You Bring Anyone In-House

An in-house program is an investment. You want to ensure high return. Here are 13 questions to ask before you ask anyone to train your trainers (or train anyone else!).

1. What kind of measurable results have other clients had from your training?
2. How much experience does this company have in training trainers?
3. Is this 100 percent of what the company does or just part of what it does?
4. How experienced are the trainers who will work with our people?
5. How experienced are your trainers in maximizing training transfer to the job?
6. Is the program tailored to my needs, or is it the same content as the public program?
7. Why is an in-house program to our advantage?
8. Is team-building a by-product of the seminar?
9. Is there immediate application of new skills during the training session?
10. What kinds of resource and reference materials do we get?
11. What type of pre-course preparation or post-course follow-up do you do?
12. How are our participants recognized for their achievements?
13. Will you teach my trainers how to get participant buy-in, even from the difficult participant?

Advantages of a Customized, In-House Program with Creative Training Techniques™ International, Inc.

Customized in-house programs provide your organization with training tailored to your specific needs. Our unique participant-centered teaching style is a revolutionary new training approach that is far more effective than traditional lecture-based training. This training approach has been adapted by a wide range of industries including healthcare, finance, communications, government, and non-profit agencies. Our clients include American Express, AT&T, Hewlett-Packard, 3M, U.S. Healthcare, and Tonka Corporation. We are eager to learn about your training needs and discuss how we can provide solutions. Please give us a call so we can help your company create a more vital and effective workforce.

1–800–383–9210
www.cttbobpike.com

Creative Training Techniques International, Inc. • 7620 W. 78th St., Mpls., MN 55439 • 612-829-1954 • Fax 612-829-0260